No End of Conflict

Also by Yossi Alpher

Periphery: Israel's Search for Middle East Allies (2015)

No End of Conflict

Rethinking Israel-Palestine

Yossi Alpher

ROWMAN & LITTLEFIELD
Lanham • Boulder • New York • London

Published by Rowman & Littlefield
A wholly owned subsidiary of The Rowman & Littlefield Publishing Group, Inc.
4501 Forbes Boulevard, Suite 200, Lanham, Maryland 20706
www.rowman.com

Unit A, Whitacre Mews, 26-34 Stannary Street, London SE11 4AB

British Library Cataloguing in Publication Information Available

Library of Congress Cataloging-in-Publication Data

Names: Alpher, Joseph, author.
Title: No end of conflict : rethinking Israel-Palestine / Yossi Alpher.
Description: Lanham ; Boulder : Rowman & Littlefield, [2016]
Identifiers: LCCN 2015036399| ISBN 9781442258587 (cloth : alk. paper) | ISBN 9781442258594
    (electronic)
Subjects: LCSH: Arab-Israeli conflict—1993– | Israel—Politics and Government—20th century. |
    Israel—Politics and government—21st century.
Classification: LCC DS119.76 .A44498 2016 | DDC 956.9405/4—dc23
    LC record available at http://lccn.loc.gov/2015036399

∞ ™ The paper used in this publication meets the minimum requirements of American
National Standard for Information Sciences Permanence of Paper for Printed Library
Materials, ANSI/NISO Z39.48-1992.

Printed in the United States of America

Contents

Maps

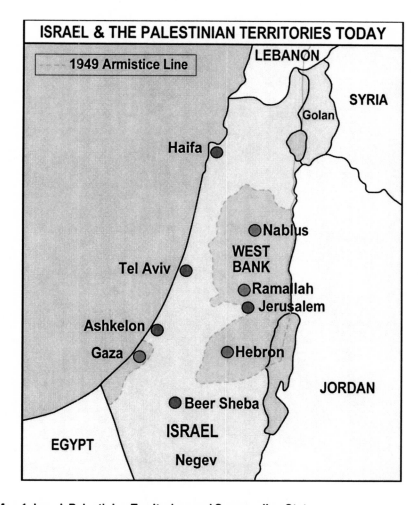

Map 1: Israel, Palestinian Territories, and Surrounding States

Maps

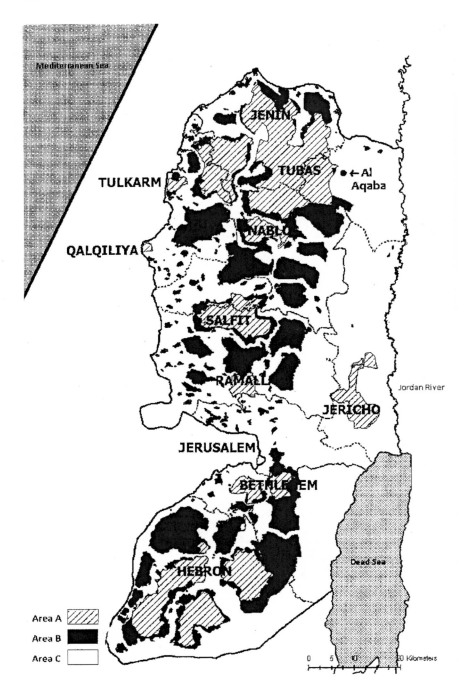

Map 2: Areas A, B, and C in the West Bank

"United Jerusalem"

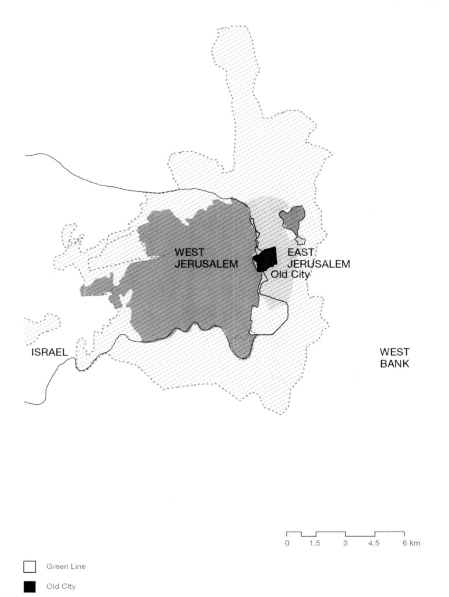

WEST
JERUSALEM

EAST
JERUSALEM
Old City

ISRAEL

WEST
BANK

0   1.5   3   4.5   6 km

Green Line

Old City

Municipal Boundary

Map 3: United Jerusalem (Source: Terrestrial Jerusalem)

Preface

In recent years, it has become increasingly clear that, despite its prosperity and inventiveness, Israel is in deep trouble. It is not only in travels to Europe and the United States that I have encountered the rhetorical query "What is happening to Israel?" Inside Israel as well, this question arises in left-wing, liberal, and moderate right-wing circles. Often it is not even a question, but rather a statement indicating a wrong direction, an inevitable crash.

Often, too, the query runs, "What in God's name is happening to Israel?" Whether intentionally or not, this suggests that a significant portion of the problem involves both Israel's religious right wing, with its messianist approach to the issues of Jerusalem, territory, and settlements, and the wave of radical Islam sweeping through Israel's neighborhood.

The year 2017 will mark the fiftieth year of Israel's occupation—or, as some would say, liberation—of Jerusalem and the West Bank. Even if Israel's current strategic situation looked far more favorable, this would be a good opportunity to examine the incredibly far-reaching and dangerous ramifications of this event for an otherwise level-headed country.

Nobody has described the situation more starkly than former Mossad head Shavtai Shavit, someone generally considered a tough right-winger, did when he wrote in the daily *Haaretz* in November 2014 that, due to "the critical mass of the threats against us on the one hand, and the government's blindness and political and strategic paralysis on the other," he was "for the first time . . . truly concerned about the future of the Zionist project."

According to Shavit, US-Israeli relations have "reached an unprecedented low point," while "Europe, our biggest market, has grown tired of us and is heading toward imposing sanctions on us. . . . We are losing the fight for support for Israel in the academic world. . . . The global BDS movement (boycott, divestment, sanctions) against Israel, which works for Israel's de-legitimization, has grown, and quite a few Jews are members." Furthermore, noted the former Mossad head, "major forces in the religious Zionist movement are foolishly doing everything they can to turn [the conflict] into the most horrific of wars, in which the entire Muslim world will stand against us."

I was an officer in Israel Defense Forces Intelligence and served in the Mossad. Perhaps that explains my propensity to cite the testimony of former security officials. To me, they, like so many retired Israel Defense

Forces generals who periodically publish petitions phrased in similar language, speak to Israel's most existential need: security in its broadest meaning.

A decade ago, at the height of the second intifada in the early years of the millennium, former security heads voiced similar protests, urging Prime Minister Ariel Sharon to take action. Sharon, their brother in arms and until then a major booster of the settlements, listened and acted to pull Israel and its settlements out of the Gaza Strip. Arguably, this became a very problematic decision in view of persistent Hamas attacks on Israel from Gaza. Yet, in a single blow, it reduced the demographic threat to Israel as a Zionist state—a major issue in this book.

Unlike Sharon, in 2014 and 2015 Prime Minister Benjamin Netanyahu, leader of the right-religious-settler establishment, did not listen—to Shavit, to the generals, or to some of his own coalition partners. Netanyahu pointed to the price Israel has paid in repeated wars with Hamas in Gaza as justification for not acting on the security establishment's advice regarding the West Bank. That there is some merit to Netanyahu's response merely underlines the quandary Israel faced by late 2015: the country is seemingly damned if it does (compromise, withdraw, bow to international pressure, entertain new dangers) and certainly damned if it doesn't (and keeps expanding settlements and driving itself willy-nilly into a one-state reality).

Netanyahu, reelected dramatically in March 2015, would undoubtedly make the case that, based on a wide variety of economic, security, and diplomatic standards, Israel is relatively well off. Significantly, the new right-wing coalition he formed in May 2015 scarcely mentioned in its official guidelines the need to resolve the Palestinian issue—an attitude without precedent since 1967. Former US president Jimmy Carter inadvertently confirmed this lacuna, stating on a visit to Jerusalem and Ramallah in April–May 2015 that prospects for renewed peace talks were so distant that he did not even discuss the matter with the Palestinian leadership (the Israeli leadership refused to meet with him). Carter, incidentally, canceled a visit to Gaza due to the threat to his life posed by Islamic State adherents there. The fate of his visit seemed to sum up rather accurately the dismal Israeli-Palestinian status quo.

Yet the absence of a peace process from the agenda should hardly be understood as diminishing the concerns of those sounding the alarm against one-statism, apartheid, and international isolation. The growing tide of criticism of Israel may be on target or totally misconceived, depending on issue areas and circumstances. But it is indeed growing, and this is extremely relevant not only for Israel but for all those affected by Israel's fortunes: Palestinians and other Arab neighbors, Europe and the United States, and Diaspora Jewry.

That is the subject of this extended essay. Its point of departure is the rising alarm among moderate Israelis and their friends and supporters and the astonishment of Israel's enemies and neutral observers regarding the ultranationalist and messianist course the country has chosen to follow: settling more and more West Bank territories and East Jerusalem neighborhoods, worsening the status of its own Arab citizens, trying to silence human rights advocates and the courts that protect them, and ignoring calls for peace, however nuanced and conditional, by the Arab world.

This book reflects an equal degree of distress with the Israeli peace camp and international peacemakers, whose approach to the issues increasingly displays a dismal ignorance of the lessons to be learned from the failure of so many attempts to resolve the conflict. The Israeli peace camp has maneuvered itself to irrelevance. The international do-gooders, with their hollow calls to "just get to the table" and their abysmally misinformed pronouncements that "the outlines of a two-state solution are obvious," were very much on my mind as I wrote.

The bottom line is a grim portrayal of the country's most likely future course. This book seeks to provide answers and explanations where possible and to define the nature of the dilemma and its consequences and ramifications where not. It does not exonerate the Palestinians, the Arab states, militant Islam, and the United States and Europe from a large portion of the blame. Its conclusions are nuanced and not unequivocal, because the entire Middle East has in recent years become more unpredictable than ever.

The knowledge and insights presented here were not achieved lightly. I have been dealing with the Palestinian issue for nearly fifty years. I did so while serving in the security establishment in the 1960s, 1970s, and 1980s. At Tel Aviv University's Jaffee Center for Strategic Studies in the 1980s and 1990s, I researched the Palestinian issue and proposed solutions, some of which influenced the peace process. In the mid-1990s, I managed to convene a series of unique meetings between the religious-ideological settler leadership from Gush Emunim and senior officials in the Palestine Liberation Organization—a frustrating experience I wrote about in 2001 in a Hebrew-language book titled *And the Wolf Shall Dwell with the Wolf: The Settlers and the Palestinians*.

Even during a five-year spell of representing the American Jewish Committee in Israel and the Middle East (1995–2000), I continued convening Israeli-Palestinian informal meetings. In July 2000, I served as special adviser to Prime Minister Ehud Barak, charged with preparing the American Jewish community and the American public in general for the tasks Washington would have to undertake in the event (which never transpired) of success in the Camp David final-status negotiations. For twelve years, beginning in 2001, I administered (together with a Palestinian partner, Ghassan Khatib) and wrote weekly for *bitterlemons*, which focused on all dimensions of the Israeli-Palestinian conflict. Since 2001, I have also written weekly on strategic issues, many of them peace process oriented, for Americans for Peace Now. (Note: I write independently and am not a member of Peace Now or of any other advocacy organization that deals with the Palestinian issue.)

This is the place to note that I, like so many of those involved over the past sixty-seven years in Israel's security and so many Israelis in general, believe strongly in the right of the Jewish people to a sovereign Jewish and democratic state in our historic homeland. I do not devote space in this book to "proving" or rationalizing that right because I view it as a fundamental principle that lies beyond the scope of a discussion of the Israeli-Palestinian conflict. However, I do recognize that many Palestinians and other Arabs, as well as some angry people elsewhere, reject this right and that, further, some Israelis are currently undermining that right by their own extremist hand. These issues I do address here.

I used to be optimistic. Then I became realistic. Now I am so concerned regarding the future that I have written this book.

Acknowledgments

This book integrates (with permission) and updates portions of several papers I wrote in recent years for the Norwegian Peacebuilding Resource Center (NOREF). It also draws on a chapter, "Israel and the US Role," that I wrote for *Pathways to Peace: America and the Arab-Israeli Conflict*, edited by Daniel C. Kurzer (2012).

I am indebted to Natasha Gill's perceptive essay "The Original 'No': Why the Arabs Rejected Zionism, and Why It Matters" (*Middle East Policy Council Commentary*, June 19, 2013), for several prestate quotes from Zionist and Palestinian leaders, and to Michael Walzer's *The Paradox of Liberation: Secular Revolution and Religious Counterrevolutions* (2015), for ideas expressed in chapter 3.

I am grateful to J. J. Goldberg, editor-at-large of *Forward*, for reading an early draft of the manuscript and offering numerous very valuable comments. As always, in writing this book I enjoyed the constant support of my wife and partner, Irene. Of course, I remain exclusively responsible for the entire contents.

Introduction

This book comprises three sections.

Chapter 1, in style and format totally unlike everything that follows, tells the true story of a very recent experience I had trying unsuccessfully to reunite an Israeli Jewish family divided since 1947 between Israel and the Palestinian population of Jordan. The failure of that endeavor sets the tone for the book.

Part I, "Contemporary Israel," looks at Israel today and seeks to explain the highly negative course Israel has embarked on. I selected the issue areas in view of their perceived effect on Israel's behavior in the Palestinian context, as I understand it. Thus, chapter 2 asks how the world sees Israel after nearly fifty years of occupation and looks back decades to debunk the nostalgic perception prevalent in many circles that things were really much better "back then." Chapter 3 examines Israel's emerging and divisive socio-political demographic composition as a challenge to its cohesiveness and capacity to reach rational but painful decisions in the Palestinian context.

There follow two chapters (4 and 5) that expand the horizon of inquiry to encompass the Jewish Diaspora, which is liable to be heavily affected by Israel's behavior toward the Palestinians, and Israel's bad Middle East neighborhood, which increasingly affects its regional perceptions and decisions. The next two chapters (6 and 7) tackle the Israeli-Palestinian peace process directly, discussing lessons from the efforts of 1936–2009 and from US Secretary of State John Kerry's failure of 2013 and 2014, at the time of writing the most recent attempt to resolve the conflict.

Part II, "Israel Tomorrow," takes as its point of departure the ultimate failure of the Oslo-based process that aimed to generate a two-state solution. Chapter 8 asks whether there are alternatives for staving off what chapters 9 and 10 describe—the slippery slope toward a binational Israel and the strategic ramifications of the quasi-apartheid schemes for Israeli society and, among other parties, Diaspora Jewry. Chapter 11 offers a cautionary concluding context regarding the difficulty of predicting the course of events in the twenty-first-century Middle East.

This is not an academic study, and there are no footnotes or references. It is an extended essay, based very much on my many years of experience dealing with the Palestinian question and its effect on Israel and including, here and there, first-person anecdotes that reflect my own insights and impressions. This book assumes the reader is leery of opinion polls, so many of which are biased, inaccurate, or ephemeral. Accordingly, I rarely cite polls and never by name; where I cite public opinion, I usually feel safe in generalizing on the basis of multiple polls. This book also assumes the reader has some basic familiarity with the issues and with the map of Israel/Palestine (though the relevant maps are provided), as well as an open mind that can contemplate the slaughtering of sacred cows, such as the widespread assumption in many quarters outside the Middle East that a compromise resolution of the conflict in the form of two states is inevitable.

A word on the spelling of names: Israel's President Rivlin transliterates his Hebrew first name with deference to the Hebrew pronunciation (Reuven, as opposed to Reuben). Prime Minister Netanyahu prefers the English Benjamin to the Hebrew Binyamin. I don't know why. But I have tried to respect their preferences and those of others, to the extent I am aware of them.

The book pays more attention to Israeli internal issues, particularly those related to the Palestinian issue, than to parallel Palestinian issues per se. This disproportion is not meant to diminish the role of the Palestinians and the Arabs in general in bringing about the current dangerous situation. Rather, it reflects my primary concern: Israel's future.

This book does not have a happy ending. Then again, it does not have a conclusive one, precisely because we are living in extremely uncertain times and discussing a region, the Middle East, where emerging new realities constantly surprise us.

ONE

Rachel, or the Arab-Jewish Divide

This is a true story, with many names and places, which have no relevance in terms of the impact of the narrative, changed for reasons of sensitivity that will become clear as it unfolds. I believe the story dramatizes clearly and at the most basic level the impasse that Israeli-Palestinian relations have reached—an impasse discussed in the remainder of the book in a far more analytical manner that hopefully explains the dissonances the story dramatizes.

In 2007 a Czech who represented a major international foundation's philanthropic activities in the Middle East contacted me by phone from Cairo, Egypt. I knew him because I had solicited funds through him for *bitterlemons*, a cooperative Arab-Israeli project I was involved in founding and maintaining. An additional reassuring factor in our acquaintance was his Jewish wife's links with Israel.

The Czech, Andreas, a heavyset guy in his forties, was calling to ask a favor. A work contact of his, a Jordanian woman named Hajar who lived in Madaba to the west of Amman, had solicited his assistance in an extremely sensitive matter. Her father had just died at a ripe old age. On his deathbed he revealed to his seven children, six sons and one daughter, now adults, that their aging mother was originally a Yemenite Jewess from Israel. Before she died, she wanted to renew ties with her family there. His dying wish was that the children help her fulfill this desire.

With the father gone, the children consulted. The sons, all Islamists of varying extremes, vehemently objected to doing anything. The daughter, Hajar, was an independent professional aged around forty and accordingly marked as something of a free spirit in conservative Arab society. Hajar defiantly announced to her family that she would take on the task.

All seven grown children were undoubtedly aware of the far-reaching consequences of the information imparted by their dying father. Their

3

mother, whom they knew as Amal and who had married their father in 1949 after, it now emerged, converting to Islam, remained Jewish in the eyes of religious Muslims and, though they might not have known it, in the eyes of at least some Jews as well. That made the children Muslim in Muslim eyes—according to Sharia, the father's religion is binding on the children—but Jewish in Jewish eyes, as under traditional Jewish law the mother passes on Jewish identity. This could be a huge problem in the increasingly Islamist environment in which they lived, dominated by Jordanians of Palestinian extraction like themselves.

As far as I could determine in the ensuing months and years, the offspring never contemplated the fact that as Jews they could now apply for Israeli citizenship and residency. Here and there, one hears of Muslim families or individuals from, say, the Caucasus or even the Gaza Strip who discover the long-suppressed identity of a Jewish parent or grandparent and seek to come to Israel as Jews. Recently a brigadier general in the Israel Defense Forces openly acknowledged having been born in Gaza to a Jewish mother and a Palestinian father. He had made his way to Israel as a young teenager following the 1967 occupation. Nothing remotely like this desire to become Israeli was to emerge in Hajar's case.

Nor did Hajar ever intimate to Andreas or to me that the task she had taken upon herself was the result of a cop-out on the part of her father. Yet he had had more than sixty years to help his wife reestablish contact; after Israel and Jordan signed a peace treaty in 1994, it was as easy as driving or flying to Israel. Instead, he chose to drop this bombshell on his children, then depart this world.

Hajar gave Andreas the following extremely limited information gleaned from her mother. Amal was born Rachel to a Yemenite Jewish family living in 1947 in the Jerusalem area. The family's last name, Ratsabi, was well known as marking them among the Yemenite Jews who had immigrated to Israel for Zionist reasons since the 1880s. Rachel's younger sister, with whom she hoped to reestablish contact, was named Sarah. Back in the days of British Mandatory Palestine, Yemenite girls did not go to school and were barely literate. Hajar recalled having several times walked in on her mother listening to the radio in what sounded like Hebrew but not being overly curious about it.

Now Hajar's mother related that she had run off to what was then Transjordan with a Palestinian boyfriend in 1947. She had lived in Jordan ever since, totally cut off from her family. Until now, telling her story to her children had been out of the question.

Could I, Andreas asked, as a favor to him, and very discreetly, try to locate the Israeli sister?

I had good reason in terms of my fund-raising needs for *bitterlemons* to do a favor for Andreas, but beyond that I immediately recognized in Hajar's request the imperative of *ichud mishpachot*, or family reunification. I felt honor bound to try. Once every few months the Israeli dailies describe reunions of brothers and sisters separated back in the 1940s by the Holocaust and brought together again half a century later. The public is treated to photos of aged siblings falling tearfully into one another's arms at Ben Gurion Airport. Here was a Middle Eastern twist on this very Jewish plot. I visited Jordan fairly regularly for conferences on Middle East issues and had good contacts there. From my standpoint, reuniting this family made perfect sense and was a *mitzvah*, a sacred duty. I am not at all religious, but accepting the challenge of bringing two long-lost sisters together, and in so doing bridging the Arab-Jewish gap, is truly a sacred duty even for a secular Jew, especially one such as myself who has long dealt with Middle East strategic affairs and particularly the Palestinian issue.

My initial inclination was to hire a private detective from an agency specializing in finding lost relatives. But first I would try the Internet, where all the cell and landline phones in the world could probably be found. Within minutes I was jotting down cellular phone numbers for every Sarah Ratsabi in Israel, on the off chance the sister was alive and still used her maiden name. The task turned out to be ridiculously easy when, on the seventh call, Sarah Ratsabi from Petah Tikva confirmed she had a sister named Rachel who had run off with an Arab boyfriend in 1947 and never been heard from again. Yes, Sarah said excitedly, she would like to be reunited with her—but discreetly. She would like to meet me to discuss how to confirm this was her sister and to bring about a reunion without anyone else knowing. Besides, she added, wasn't this potentially dangerous? Could her Jordanian family be a bunch of terrorists? She also sounded unfocused—not a good omen.

I reported back to Andreas and got the go-ahead to meet Sarah and, when necessary, to talk directly by phone to Hajar in Madaba. Sarah, not to my surprise, insisted she couldn't meet me at her home lest the neighbors get wind of her "Arab family." We would have to meet in my car, on a street near where she lived. Worried by her apparent paranoia, I asked whether she could perhaps bring her children or other family into the picture. "Absolutely impossible," she replied. I sensed that I was dealing with a suspicious woman well on in years and began to fear lest Sarah's concerns were somehow gender based. So I recruited my wife to accompany me to the first encounter.

Late one rainy winter night on a deserted Petah Tikva street, we ushered Sarah into our car. We encountered a dysfunctional woman: semicoherent, unkempt, and hard put to keep it all together. Still, considering that she had to be over seventy, she looked young for her years. She related that she had been deserted long ago by her husband, lived on social security, and had a daughter with whom she was not on speaking terms. Contacting the daughter—it seemed to make sense to let the two cousins, Hajar and Sarah's daughter, Shlomit, take over this entire project—was, Sarah insisted, out of the question.

Having an Arab sibling, Sarah intimated, was a nightmare, but family is family, and if we could keep this quiet, Sarah would like to verify that Rachel was her sister. She provided photos of their father and mother and an old postcard with a photo of Marlene Dietrich on one side and on the other a nondescript message of regards written in barely literate Hebrew by Rachel before she disappeared. I undertook to scan them, send them via Andreas to Hajar, and seek confirmation from the Jordanian side.

Within days, Rachel/Amal had agreed on the basis of this limited documentation that she and Sarah could conceivably be sisters. Working by phone and e-mail with Andreas, then directly with Hajar, we arranged that the two sisters would talk by phone. Hajar was, as advertised by Andreas, intelligent, sophisticated, and fluent in English—a far cry from her presumed Israeli aunt. But she emphasized that heavy fears and hesitations existed on her end as well. Since her brothers aggressively opposed the entire effort on behalf of their mother, the conversation would have to take place when none of her siblings and none of her mother's many grandchildren were around. After phoning back and forth with Sarah and Hajar, we set a time, late one evening. Again, our family car would host a cell phone conversation from the Israeli end, and my wife would come along.

The phone reunion between the two sisters after a fifty-nine-year separation was a disaster. Sarah had assured me she knew some Arabic from her childhood growing up in a Yemeni family; Rachel had assured Hajar she remembered Hebrew. In the crunch, neither sister could speak more than two words in the other's language. Hajar and I took over the conversation, in English, each translating for a sister. Sarah asked Rachel two questions about their father; Rachel's replies, after translation from Arabic to English to Hebrew, disappointed Sarah. Sarah mentioned a brother who had died in infancy; Rachel said that was impossible.

"She's not my sister," Sarah pronounced. In Madaba, in parallel, Hajar's mother now claimed that the purported photos of her parents "did not belong to her." She was, according to Hajar, "more scared than ever" about the entire project. Neither sister would agree to a DNA test.

Hajar seemed anxious to drop the entire matter: "What else can we do if it doesn't work?" she asked me in a brief phone conversation. "We simply forget about everything and go on with our lives as if this never happened. The situation is too complicated." I reminded myself that for Hajar, dealing with a Jewish link in her family could conceivably be physically dangerous if colleagues and possibly even family members with Islamist tendencies found out. To be on the safe side, I continued going through my initial phone list of Sarah Ratsabis, calling them all just in case I was wrong about this particular Sarah and there was another match. There was not.

Again I suggested to Sarah that she contact her estranged daughter, Shlomit, and let the cousins, if indeed they were cousins, deal with this. I emphasized to Sarah that I had no interest in being involved, beyond the minimum necessary, in what I knew was a painful and sensitive family matter. I would step aside at the first opportunity if Sarah wanted to continue or to bring her daughter into the picture. Sarah refused to discuss her estranged daughter. After further consultations with Hajar in Madaba and Andreas in Amman, we agreed reluctantly to drop the matter for lack of a way forward.

The Ratsabi family of Madaba and Petah Tikva seemed to be an overwhelming challenge. I was disappointed but, having plenty of things to keep me busy, soon put the whole affair behind me.

A year went by. One day, out of the blue, I got a call from Shlomit, who introduced herself as Sarah's daughter. She and her mother had reconciled. Sarah had told her the story. She wanted to pursue the matter of her Palestinian Jordanian family. Could I brief her on what had transpired and hand over the few family articles that had remained in my possession?

She came to my house in Ramat HaSharon on a Saturday afternoon with her daughter, a high school student who, refreshingly, found the entire affair intriguing and exciting. Shlomit, a petite, intense professional woman in her forties and a senior bank official, was businesslike. Family is family, and the attempt to reunite her mother and her aunt had to be pursued. While, happily, she did not share her mother's hang-up about the neighbors finding out, she also wanted to maintain discretion. Still, it was a relief to find that the younger generation of Ratsabis, on both sides of the Jordan River, had a modern and liberal outlook.

We discussed ways a meeting could be arranged: in Israel, by obtaining visas for Rachel and Hajar at the Israel embassy in Amman; in Madaba or Amman or even at the Amman international airport or a nearby hotel, with Shlomit and Sarah getting their Jordanian visas wherever they chose to enter Jordan, on land or by air—a far simpler process than for Jordanians wishing to visit Israel.

Wasn't it dangerous to visit there? Shlomit asked. I replied that I had traveled to and via Jordan many times. Discretion was advised about broadcasting one's Israeli identity, but Israeli tourists did visit. Come to think of it, the two families could arrange to meet at Petra in the southern Jordanian desert, one of the seven wonders of the ancient world, or the Red Sea port of Aqaba, adjacent to Israel's Eilat; both are tourist sites frequented by Israelis. If they still hesitated, they could easily meet in Cyprus, the nearest neutral country with ties to both Israel and Jordan. Getting together really should not be a problem.

I reiterated to Shlomit what I had already told her mother and Hajar: that I would happily butt out of their family's secrets if they would take on the project. I e-mailed Hajar and informed her that Shlomit, probably her cousin, was taking over at the Israeli end. Hajar agreed to "one more try." Equipped with her cousin Hajar's phone numbers in Madaba, Shlomit decided to contact her. Whether she would keep me abreast of progress was not made clear. When I heard no more, I assumed that Shlomit had everything under control and I would never know how the family reunion transpired.

Four more years passed during which the entire Middle East descended into the chaos of revolution and counterrevolution mistakenly labeled the "Arab Spring." I had long forgotten the Ratsabi family reunion project.

Then, in October 2013, Shlomit phoned. She needed urgent advice. On the one hand, she and Hajar had, through phone and Skype conversations, long ago concluded with certainty that they were first cousins. On the other, nothing further had happened since we last met; both sides had been too frightened to consummate a meeting. But now Rachel's health was deteriorating, and they couldn't wait any longer. Rachel was unable to travel abroad. Hajar had tried to request a visa for herself at the Israel consulate in Amman, but the security, the endless forms, and the questions had put her off. These were indeed known to be daunting: Israel feared Palestinian citizens of Jordan who were 1948 refugees and wanted to "make return" or who might belong to terrorist organizations. Sarah and Shlomit would have to travel to Jordan.

"What stopped you over the past four years?" I asked. Fear, was Shlomit's answer. Weren't people threatening Israel in Jordan? "Who?" I asked. She didn't remember. "It's an Arab country. I'm afraid to go there. They were afraid to come here. Now what do we do? Can you help us get to Jordan? You know the ropes. Will you come with us? My mother wants you to come. Please. We're running out of time. The two sisters are very old."

Is this entire family dysfunctional, I asked myself, on both sides of the Jordan River? Or are they just regular people who have become immersed, after decades of Arab-Israel conflict, in fear and prejudice? Then again, perhaps those two characterizations are really one and the same. I contacted an Israeli friend, Meir, who had once helped me with some delicate arrangements in Jordan when I came to Amman to attend a conference and who had close government contacts there.

Israeli-Jordanian relations, I knew, had seen better days since a peace treaty was signed in 1994. The unsolved and unsolvable Palestinian issue constituted a mighty thorn in the side of King Abdullah II, a savvy young monarch ruling over a population roughly half Palestinian. Abdullah was bound both by destiny—as a Hashemite, he is a direct descendant of the Prophet Muhammed—and by the peace treaty, which awards him responsibility for Muslim holy sites under Israeli control in Jerusalem, to object loudly to the activities of messianist Israelis who insisted on trying to change the status of the Temple Mount and engage in Jewish prayer there. Located in the heart of Jerusalem, the Mount, known to Muslims as Haram al-Sharif (the Noble Sanctuary), contains the long-buried ruins of the ancient Jewish temples but also holds two mosques that constitute the third-holiest site of Islam. Relations had deteriorated even further in view of the stalemated Israeli-Palestinian peace process and under the pressure of Islamists dominating the Jordanian "street."

Only security contacts were in good shape—both Israel and Jordan feared the same revolutionary Islamists in Syria and Iraq—but this could have no bearing on my mission. When I explained the family-reunification issue at stake to Meir, I added that the behavior of both branches of the family seemed to be problematic and that I assumed this was a bad time for him in view of the mood in Jordan. I told him I would understand if he backed off from helping.

Instead, he plunged in, intrigued by the Ratsabi family narrative and, like me, impelled to help get Rachel and Sarah back together after a separation now reaching sixty-six years. He would use his contacts in Amman and arrange for Sarah, Shlomit, and me to enter Jordan via the Allenby Bridge, now known as the King Hussein Bridge. Allenby, linking Jordan with the West Bank, was usually open only to Palestinians heading for Jordan and to third-country nationals and was out of bounds to nonofficial Israelis, who were obliged to enter Jordan from sovereign Israeli territory to the north or south. Meir would arrange a trusty driver for us for the day, someone who had worked with him for years. He suggested we meet in a hotel lobby, either in Amman or on the Jordanian Dead Sea coast.

Again I passed command of the operation back to Shlomit. She would contact my friend, provide passport information needed for the Allenby crossing, and coordinate the meeting in Jordan with Hajar and her mother. Hajar agreed to one of the Jordanian Dead Sea hotel lobbies for the meeting. This made sense: the hotels were near the Allenby Bridge and offered whatever facilities we might need. The two cousins, Hajar and Shlomit, picked a date in December 2013.

A one-day round trip, Israel-Jordan-Israel, via Allenby was easy logistically, as long as the arrangements worked and there were no hitches. The drive to Allenby from my home near Tel Aviv early in the morning would take ninety minutes. Passport and customs inspection on both sides, once all the fees were paid and assuming bureaucratic arrangements had been properly handled, would take another ninety minutes. Half an hour by car to the Dead Sea. Two hours at the hotel for the family reunion. The same procedures coming back. That left several hours for snags and bureaucratic delays before the bridge crossing closed for the night.

But who could predict how the meeting would go? There might be hysterics in the hotel lobby—old women screaming accusations or even, in a best-case scenario, crying for joy and attracting unwanted attention.

My participation, demanded by Sarah, might prove unwanted by the Jordanian women. I made preparations for potential problems by taking with me the business cards and phone numbers of every high-level Jordanian I knew: retired generals, diplomats, scholars. I stuffed wads of Jordanian dinars, US dollars, and euros into my briefcase the night before. Who knew what debacle I might have to bail us out of.

I was keyed up: years of effort were about to come to fruition in the meeting of the sisters and cousins. In reflecting on seven years of this Ratsabi family project with my wife, who, after all, had been there from the outset, I realized that for me this was about more than reuniting family members separated in circumstances that paralleled the entire history of Arab-Israel wars and estrangement. In December 2013, with the Middle East in chaos, no hope for peace, no hope for a two-state solution, every likelihood of more war with Gaza and of terrorism in general, and the next round of elections almost certain to leave ultranationalist reactionaries in power in Israel, getting Rachel and Sarah back together and cementing a bond between Hajar and Shlomit was the closest I might ever come to helping bring about family-level Palestinian-Israeli reconciliation. My wife noted that, with one day to go, I had become more emotionally committed to this enterprise than the two dysfunctional, fear-obsessed families on both sides of the Jordan.

Late that night, as I made final preparations, Shlomit phoned. Hajar had called her tearfully to cancel the next day's meeting. Until that evening she had not told her siblings about the reunion plan. Now apparently she had to, since she was taking her mother out for the day. Her brothers responded with anger; they even threatened her if she went through with it. Meeting with Israelis was too dangerous. Among other things, my participation at Sarah's behest was understood as a Mossad plot.

I groaned with frustration. I should not have been surprised. "Why not limit the meeting just to you and Hajar?" I suggested to Shlomit in a last-ditch effort to keep this reunion alive. "You can do this on your own, Shlomit. I'll even come with you to the bridge and help you hook up to Meir's Jordanian driver."

"I suggested that just Hajar and I meet," Shlomit replied. "Hajar said she'd get back to me. Now she won't answer her phone." Shlomit hesitated a few seconds, then sighed and said, "The last thing Hajar said to me was, 'This is a place of fear.'"

Part I

Contemporary Israel

TWO

After Nearly Fifty Years of Occupation

How the World Increasingly Sees Israel

"A shitty little country" was the ugly way a former French ambassador to the United Kingdom described it in an ill-advised dinner-table remark in London back in 2001, a comment blown to scandalous proportions around Tel Aviv and Jerusalem dinner tables. The remark was neither nice nor necessary. But it certainly summed up the way more and more Europeans and Americans see Israel.

Nearly fifty years of occupation of the West Bank and East Jerusalem, at times as "enlightened" as occupations go but increasingly seen by most of the world and not a few Israelis as oppressive, is the most obvious explanation for this view. But it is by far not the only one: a case can be made that growing anger and resentment toward Israel also reflect rising Arab influence on the international scene, Islamist influence in Europe and elsewhere, general support for the Palestinian "underdog" (regardless of whether its approach is sensible), an exaggerated international law and human rights approach to Israel's wars that ignores their unique circumstances, and, here and there without doubt, anti-Semitism.

Certainly a case can be made that the international community exercises a double standard, ignores Palestinian rejection of reasonable Israeli offers in 2000 and 2008 of a two-state solution, ignores the 2005 unilateral withdrawal from Gaza that for the first time gave the Palestinians a degree of sovereignty over finite territory, and ignores the Palestinian response: suicide bombers, rockets, and tunnels.

But occupation is the clincher: even the most powerful reasoning cannot explain it away.

One undeniable source of growing international disapproval of Israel is the behavior of its increasingly dominant messianist, ultranationalist,

13

pro-settler political factions. The settlement landgrab and repeated extremist Jewish initiatives to suppress human rights among Israel's own Arab minority through demands for loyalty oaths, relegation of Arabic to secondary status, and crowning of Israel as exclusively the "nation state of the Jewish people," along with instances of collective punishment in the West Bank, a fanatic minority's campaign to reestablish a Jewish religious presence on the Temple Mount, and the far-reaching denial of equal development opportunities to the huge Palestinian minority in "united Jerusalem"—all contribute to this negative image. In fact, many of these injustices pertained even under Israeli governments led by the political Left and Center after 1967, but at the time the parallel existence of sincere attempts to reach an agreed political solution to the Palestinian issue (under Yitzhak Rabin, Shimon Peres, Ehud Barak, and Ehud Olmert) mitigated the impact. So did Ariel Sharon's readiness to withdraw unilaterally from Gaza and a small portion of the West Bank.

Many of the extremist initiatives noted above, including loyalty oaths, were ultimately never enacted as legislation, having been defeated by a still-lucid and rational but shrinking political majority. Yet the latter can no longer sustain its vision of two states for two peoples. This is due not only to the bombastic Israeli Right but also to a Palestinian leadership incapable of compromising where realism demands, an Israeli political Left that is at times highly unrealistic about both the prospects for peace and the mechanics of attaining it, and the deadening effect on Israeli-Palestinian coexistence of the threats posed by militant and uncompromising Islamists in the surrounding region, particularly those increasingly gathering right on Israel's borders.

Human rights are still broadly observed in Israel. The Israel Defense Forces (IDF) still fight as morally and ethically as any army involved on behalf of a democratic country in seemingly endless warfare for nearly seventy years (there is no other, so comparisons are useless). Yet you wouldn't know it for all the biased media coverage Israel gets. As journalist Mati Friedman demonstrated in 2014, recounting, example by example, his experiences working for the Associated Press's Jerusalem bureau, much of the international media and many global human rights organizations devote highly exaggerated coverage to Israel and seemingly exult in displaying Jews as examples of moral failure and symbols of militarism, colonialism, and racism, while holding Palestinians and other Arabs to a much lower moral and democratic standard. "Jews with power," Friedman concludes, seemingly deserve particularly critical treatment at the international level.

We could go on. On the one hand, David has become Goliath, and Israelis with their Holocaust preoccupation seem to expect special treatment internationally. The threat of political boycott and economic sanctions, particularly on the part of European countries, is growing. More and more of them are recognizing a virtual Palestinian state and threatening Israel with isolation.

On the other hand—and here I invite the reader to tolerate a brief excursion into Israeli self-justification, if only to ensure a degree of symmetry and balance in what follows—Israel has as much right to declare itself a Jewish state as England, Sweden, and Denmark have to be Christian states, twenty-five countries to be Muslim states, and four to be Buddhist states. The "start-up nation" can brag of growing trade and strategic dialogue with Russia, India, China, and even the very European Union that threatens it with sanctions. Its relations with the moderate Sunni Arab states have never been better, even if those ties remain largely clandestine and deniable. Around ten thousand Jews are immigrating to Israel annually from Western countries where militant Islam is on the rise.

If Israel fights its wars disproportionately and even brutally, this is because it has to win all its wars—even the seemingly unjust ones—in order to maintain its deterrence of existential threats from Iran and Sunni Islamists. Even civilized countries that do not have to win all their wars, and sometimes don't, like the United States, end up inadvertently inflicting heavy civilian casualties when engaged in asymmetric conflict with nonstate actors that embed themselves in civilian populations. The international community could stop applying suspicious double standards and cut Israel some slack, just as Egypt, Jordan, and Saudi Arabia do. Just as Friedman makes a good case that negative treatment of Israel by the international media is exaggerated and unwarranted, others, such as American scholar Joshua Muravchik and Israeli journalist Ben-Dror Yemini, point out that a considerable portion of the criticism of Israel by parties ranging from Jimmy Carter to international and even Israeli human rights groups is often grossly inaccurate.

Yet this discussion is increasingly pointless, because the bottom line is simple: in the twenty-first century, you can't occupy another people for nearly fifty years, leave it stateless and under varying degrees of military rule, and expect the world to acquiesce. This is particularly true if you are a small country that belongs to no global political bloc and has few, if any, real friends. You can rationalize your occupation strategy in a thousand clever ways and explain that the Palestinians are a terrible partner for a viable and peaceful two-state solution, but after fifty years the rationales wear thin. You can withdraw unilaterally from the Gaza Strip, asking nothing in return and encouraging the West Bank–based Palestinian leadership to take charge there and the international community to invest, and you'll still be blamed as an "occupier" when they all fail spectacularly at state-building.

Would ending the West Bank occupation in a convincing way change this? Or would the growing chorus of critics of Israel internationally remain in attack mode? And would the boycott, divestment, and sanctions movement, with its antioccupation rank and file but hard core of activists who seek Israel's total disappearance, find ways to continue the anti-Israel campaign? First of all, even if Israel tries, finding a "convincing way" might be hard since Israel's legitimate security needs in defending its tiny territory will for a long time to come provide grist for the mill of those detractors who insist that elements of occupation continue to prevail. Second, we will only know if we try and succeed. Or at least try. As matters stand, we are not really trying.

THE GOOD OLD DAYS BEFORE 1967

Israel's growing isolation and lack of popularity in some international circles, coupled with concerted criticism by the country's shrinking liberal left-wing sector and growing unease among majority centrists, have generated a nostalgia phenomenon. Israel, the critics say, is not what it used to be: liberal, tolerant, interested only in defending itself, ready to make peace at any price. The good old days, usually described as extending from Israel's founding in 1948 to the aftermath of the 1967 Six-Day War, have become a standard for judging the country's many faults today.

And without doubt, it has many faults. But is the country really in such bad shape compared to the past? Are founding fathers like David Ben Gurion and founding documents like the 1948 Declaration of Independence, which is remarkable for its liberal values and peace-oriented language, really the standard against which Israel looks so bad these days? Here a reminder of pre-1967 Israel is in order.

From 1949 to 1966, the Arab citizens of Israel lived under military rule. An Arab wishing to travel anywhere outside his or her town or village needed a permit from a military governor. Road signs were not bilingual, in Hebrew and Arabic. Few Arabs went to university, and few, if any, taught at the university level. The state routinely took over land belonging to or claimed by Arabs in order to accommodate Jewish housing. Arabs were not integrated into the country's economy, which in any case was fairly primitive.

One reason it was primitive was its quasi-Bolshevik management. Centralization and central planning were key. An oppressive bureaucracy and a culture of handwritten "notes" and tax stamps needed to get anything done hamstrung independent business initiatives. The huge waves of immigration, often from relatively underdeveloped areas of eastern Europe and North Africa, generated a need for massive state-sponsored employment and housing projects that dominated budgets. Behind it all, all too often, were officials with no idea whatsoever of bureaucratic efficiency and no professional qualifications, generating a situation in which an individual doing business with the government devoted days to moving from official to official, all the while collecting paperwork. The currency was constantly devalued; as late as 1984, annual inflation stood at 400 percent.

The all-encompassing Histadrut labor confederation and Jewish Agency immigration and absorption bureaucracies constituted governments within the government. So did the Labor Party in its earlier manifestation as Mapai, whose monopolistic rule only began to dissipate in 1967. As late as 1973, Prime Minister Golda Meir was talking politburo style about prioritizing "the party" over the government. The bureaucratic and patronage-heavy Histadrut monopolized health care. Dependent new immigrants were easily bamboozled into voting for the ruling socialists.

Travel abroad required clearance by the army (for military-age men and women) and payment by all citizens of a heavy exit tax. Leaving the country for good was stigmatized as "descending" (immigration to Israel was "ascending"). Yet many scraped together the money to leave, if only because the country was asphyxiating them.

The kibbutzim, Israel's poster child, clung jealously to collective practices that may have seemed necessary in the nation-building phase of the first half of the twentieth century but became increasingly anachronistic year by year. Youth growing up in the kibbutzim or settled in them by well-meaning welfare authorities were not free to pursue higher education or to choose their workplace. If, like myself, you arrived at a kibbutz with a university degree in Oriental studies, the kibbutz elders informed you that your destiny was to be a high school chemistry teacher. Women, supposed to be equal members of an egalitarian society, mostly did the washing up and laundry for the entire collective community. "Ideological collectivity" dictated that all kibbutz residents vote for the same socialist party, read the same newspaper, and even sing the same songs.

The European Jewish establishment stigmatized as primitive the eastern Jews who arrived in large numbers from the Arab world, Iran, and Turkey during the 1950s and settled them far from urban cultural and educational centers, on the "periphery," in "development towns." Orthodox and ultra-Orthodox Jews were relatively few and were marginalized. But not their culture: the Orthodox rabbinate controlled marriage and divorce, and kosher food had to be served in state institutions. Theaters, cinemas, restaurants, and cafés were closed even in the most secular communities on Saturday, the Jewish Sabbath.

The country began in 1948 with three university-level institutions. For decades there were no think tanks, and study of foreign cultures was limited, with the exception of Middle East culture, knowledge of which was important to the security community. Talk of human rights and civil rights was in its infancy, despite the guarantees of Israel's Declaration of Independence. The prime minister, usually David Ben Gurion, briefed newspaper editors regarding what they could and could not, should and should not, write, and they obeyed. The Shin Bet internal security service spied on the Far Left and Far Right parties of the Zionist political spectrum, not to mention the communists and the Arabs.

There was no television. Ben Gurion's education minister, Zalman Aran, prohibited the Beatles from coming to Israel to perform, lest they corrupt the youth. Young Israelis addicted to Western pop music were obliged to listen to a radio station beaming from Ramallah in the West Bank, then part of Jordan. The country was economically isolated: there were no relations with India and China, and an Arab economic boycott deterred international brands like Coca-Cola and Toyota from entering the Israeli market. That Israel offered extensive agricultural and community-organization aid to newly emerging African countries was a ray of light.

The Israel Defense Forces defended the country against Arab enemies who openly sought its destruction. Accordingly, violations of the "purity of arms"—the code of moral conduct for military activities—were tolerated and occasionally even glorified: slaughter of transient Bedouin in the Negev, needless killing of civilians in cross-border raids, even the sporadic murder of prisoners of war. In recently released recordings, decommissioned kibbutzniks discussed their Six-Day War experiences of needlessly killing surrendering enemy soldiers. An IDF chief of staff who seduced the wives of his subordinate officers and stole antique artifacts from archeological digs was a national hero.

It's easy to dismiss all this as folklore. Were these not simply the foibles of an infant state surrounded by enemies, still reeling from the death and destruction of a war for survival in 1948, just beginning to come to terms with the meaning of the Holocaust in the context of the sweep of Jewish history, suspicious of an Arab enemy within, overwhelmed by the influx of immigrants and isolated internationally? The hardship and narrow horizons were balanced by an egalitarian ethos (ethos only, and only among the socialist elite; there was plenty of corruption, but few ways existed to monitor and expose it), a genuine pioneering spirit, and grassroots patriotism. Foundations were being laid for an admirable effort to integrate eastern Jews and even Arabs, for broadly accessible higher education, for high-tech agriculture and industry, all of which would blossom within a generation or two.

Israel had the highest rate of immigrant absorption in the world, doubling its Jewish population in its first four years. Even the rate of "reimmigration," or departure by immigrants, was low by comparison to more prosperous immigrant-absorbing countries like Canada and New Zealand. The status of women and minorities, and even the bureaucracy of government and the behavior of the IDF, were fairly unremarkable by the international standards of the day. As the country approaches a mere seventy years of existence, it has a lot to be proud of in these highly constrained roots.

But to be nostalgic about? Today Israel is less corrupt and far more liberal. Tel Aviv, an international gay capital, runs its cafés and places of entertainment 24/7, and it's hard to find a kosher restaurant outside the hotels. Women fly combat aircraft and run large parts of the economy. Jews of eastern origin head the army and police; one was president until he was convicted of rape and sent to jail (not many countries dare put their president on trial). IDF combat units fight shoulder to shoulder with lawyers who advise them on which methods of fighting are ethical and which aren't. Arabs are increasingly integrated into the judicial system, academia, medicine, pharmacy, and mass communications. Members of the Druze minority hold senior officer positions in the army. Over the most recent decades, voters have rotated political leadership among parties of the Right, Left, and Center. Many political parties are run by their members, not, as they once were, by aging apparatchiks in smoke-filled rooms. And yes, smoking is banned in public places. Health care is competitive and excellent.

I am nostalgic about earlier Israeli life in only one aspect. Prior to 1967 we did not occupy the West Bank and Gaza with their millions of Palestinians. There was no "Palestinian problem"—only an Arab problem. Messianism, if it existed, was not directed at holy places but instead focused, Tolstoy-style, on physical labor, defense of the country, and absorption of immigrants as means of redeeming the Jewish people. The West Bank and East Jerusalem were called "Jordan." Israel enjoyed a relatively unified national sense of purpose.

When we very legitimately defended ourselves and won the June 1967 Six-Day War, the world we cared about, the world of Western civilization and Diaspora Jewry, still loved us. The only fly in the ointment was French president Charles de Gaulle's severance of military cooperation and admonition about our arrogance. Perhaps we should have paid more attention. But the world still more or less loved us ten years later, following a second all-out war and the beginnings of peace with Egypt.

The peace treaty Israel signed with Egypt in March 1979 was a critical first step toward implementing United Nations Security Council Resolution 242 of 1967, which laid out the parameters of "territories for peace." Back then, 242 never mentioned the Palestinians because they were not considered a relevant actor in the Arab-Israel drama. And it ignored the anomalous status of the West Bank and Gaza—territories not under the recognized sovereignty of any country. Nor did more than a handful of Israelis anticipate the effect the conquest and occupation of those lands would have on Israeli society. We shall return to these themes in chapters 3 and 6. For now, it is sufficient to note that any analysis of the present situation and projection of scenarios for the future will be seriously flawed if it falls back on a false idealization of the past.

THREE

The Emerging Social-Political-Demographic Challenge to Israeli Internal Cohesion

Pluralism and diversity are positive attributes in any society, but only as long as there exist enough threads of commonality and consensus, preferably spearheaded by a dominant but tolerant majority, to maintain a broadly uniform sense of purpose. In Israel of 2015, all these qualities and characteristics are threatened. Consequently, the capacity of the Israeli body politic to make coherent decisions regarding existential issues like the Palestinian question has been seriously compromised.

Israel no longer enjoys a broadly uniform sense of purpose. Pluralism is getting out of hand, and consensus is lost when an Arab minority of nearly 20 percent increasingly and vocally rejects the raison d'être of the state as a Jewish homeland. Affluent and secular Tel Aviv is liberal; Jerusalem and nearly all the rest of the country are conservative. There is no clear majority—certainly not a tolerant one—when a significant minority of messianist Jews, empowered by emerging religious nationalist elites (comprising only some 12 percent of the population but wielding "values" that attract another large percentage), attains enough political influence to drive the state, albeit from a totally different point of departure than that of the Israeli Arab minority, toward self-immolation as a Jewish homeland.

Meanwhile, the liberal "peace camp" is becoming increasingly marginalized among the Tel Aviv elites, hence bereft of influence. Tensions between it and the political Right led by Prime Minister Benjamin Netanyahu, which is now firmly established as the mainstream, proliferate—over cultural issues, socioeconomic issues, and peace-related issues—and are becoming increasingly strident and ugly, with each side falling back on incendiary rhetoric to characterize the other and its public supporters and voters. The country's income gap, too, is growing to extreme proportions, with mainly Arabs, ultra-Orthodox Jews, and some right-wing voters sharing the lower socioeconomic brackets.

The roots of this growing challenge to the country's internal cohesiveness can be traced, first and foremost, to the outcome of the 1967 Six-Day War, specifically to the conquest and ensuing occupation by Israel nearly fifty years ago of East Jerusalem, the West Bank, and the Gaza Strip. That war found Israeli politics, as they had been since 1948, divided among a labor/pragmatist "founding fathers" ruling mainstream (note: it harbored a small Greater Land of Israel faction), a revisionist-secular ultranationalist parliamentary opposition led by Menachem Begin (brought into the governing coalition at the last minute before the 1967 war), Orthodox religious Zionists (until 1967 moderate centrists), and ultra-Orthodox non-Zionists. Its outcome affected internal Israel in critical ways.

OCCUPATION AND SETTLEMENT

The conquest of the West Bank and East Jerusalem ignited a messianist fervor primarily among Orthodox Israeli Jews who took the lead in what appeared to them as the logical next phase of Zionist settlement of the land. For the first time, the Zionist movement controlled more than relatively minor Jewish sites of historical and religious importance in pre-1967 Israel (like the Eila Valley, where David smote Goliath, and tombs of the late Second Temple and early Talmudic sages in the Galilee). Now it controlled the most hallowed sites of all: the Western Wall and Temple Mount in the Old City of Jerusalem, the graves of the Patriarchs in Hebron, the site of the first location of the Ark of the Covenant at Shiloh, and all the places where the heroes of the Old Testament walked, fought their wars, and even argued with God.

These sites, all on the high ground of the West Bank mountain ridge, already held a large and growing population of Palestinian Arabs who, for the most part, were not displaced by the recent war, unlike the vast numbers displaced in 1948 from what became Israel. But settlers did not allow this fact to constitute a lasting impediment.

Because settlers and the settlement movement are so central both to the issue of Israeli internal cohesion and to the Israeli-Palestinian question, a brief discussion of them is in order. The nature of the Jewish settler movement in the West Bank in 2015 is best understood in the context of the relevant historical, legal, and ideological backdrop.

THE SETTLERS: HISTORICAL BACKDROP

The West Bank (known in Israel also by the biblical names Judea and Samaria) is the heartland of the biblical Hebrew kingdoms. That it was not the primary focus of Jewish settlement in Palestine during the early decades of modern Zionism is explained by the large Arab population there and consequently the availability of land for purchase and settlement by Jews primarily on the malaria-ridden coastal strip, in the northern Negev and in the Galilee. West Bank Arab towns and cities are concentrated mainly on the mountain spine that runs from north to south, where altitude made for a healthier climate even in biblical times and where elevation has offered the best conditions for defense from invaders since premodern times.

The Gaza Strip is, from a traditional Jewish standpoint, not part of the Land of Israel and was accordingly not a focus of Jewish settlement until after the 1967 Six-Day War, when security requirements vis-à-vis its Palestinian population and its neighbor Egypt were perceived to mandate settlement there designed to fragment the Palestinian population and block a land offensive by Egypt.

Prior to Israel's 1948 War of Independence, there were West Bank Jewish settlements at Gush Etzion near Bethlehem, near the Dead Sea, and north of Jerusalem. All were evacuated during the 1948 war. After surrendering, the defenders of Gush Etzion were massacred by the Jordanian Arab Legion—an act that made this region the natural first choice for post-1967 Jewish settlement in the West Bank. A Jewish community existed for centuries in Hebron, traditionally Abraham's home and King David's first capital, until it was decimated by a pogrom in 1929. This also explains why Hebron was one of the first West Bank settlements after 1967.

OCCUPIED TERRITORIES, LIBERATED TERRITORIES, AND EAST JERUSALEM

Under international law, the West Bank and East Jerusalem are occupied territories, having been captured by Israel from Jordan in 1967. Israeli governments have disputed this characterization, noting that Jordanian sovereignty in the territory was never internationally recognized and that, accordingly, these territories did not really belong to anybody. Hence, according to this interpretation—which is not accepted by any other state but certainly has some basis in a literal reading of paragraph two of the Fourth Geneva Convention of 1949—the West Bank's provenance is disputed, and under the 1993 Oslo Accords, its disposition should be the subject of negotiations with the Palestine Liberation Organization (PLO).

Settler and other right-wing groups in Israel prefer the term "liberated territories" for the West Bank, thereby indicating their intention eventually to apply Israeli sovereignty there. Israeli governments usually call them "disputed." The Israel Defense Forces' (IDF) presence and ultimate direct or indirect control over the territories in their entirety renders these zones "occupied" in the eyes of the world and their inhabitants.

One way or another, a succession of Israeli governments has deemed pre-1967 Jordanian "crown" or state land in the West Bank to be available for Israeli settlement at the initiative of the current crown, Israel. Because land-ownership delineation was incomplete prior to the 1967 conquest, a number of settlements are built on disputed land; on rare occasions, the Israel High Court of Justice has mandated returning these lands to Palestinian owners. Usually, Israeli government and military officials sympathetic to the settlers help them to skirt these mandates bureaucratically. After nearly fifty years of occupation, approximately 10 percent of Israel's Jewish population (around 600,000 out of some 6 million) lives across the green line (the 1948 armistice line with Jordan) in East Jerusalem and the West Bank.

A similar controversy regarding jurisdiction surrounded the Gaza Strip—which from 1948 to 1967 was occupied by Egypt but, unlike in the case of the West Bank and Jordan, never annexed by Egypt—until Israel withdrew both the settler and the IDF presence in 2005. Since then, Israel claims it no longer can be seen as occupying Gaza, while many in the international community insist it is still an occupier insofar as it controls most of Gaza's borders and its air and naval space. In any event, Gaza, since 2007 under Hamas rule and periodically at war with Israel, is no longer a settlement-related issue. Yet it and its approximately 1.8 million Palestinian inhabitants remain very much a component of a projected two-state solution, and the status of its border crossings with Israel, which the IDF monitors heavily due to security considerations, continues to attract global attention.

Israel annexed what is called East Jerusalem, which it captured from Jordan in the Six-Day War, in June 1967. In fact, the large area annexed and included within the expanded boundaries of Israel's capital city lies to the north, east, and south of pre-1967 Jewish West Jerusalem and the adjacent Arab East Jerusalem. The Israeli annexation has never been recognized internationally; yet Israel insists that the more than 200,000 Jews settled in the annexed areas of the vastly enlarged city (alongside 300,000 Palestinian residents of East Jerusalem) enjoy a different status from the nearly 400,000 West Bank settlers, who live among some 2.5 million Palestinians in the West Bank.

At the heart of united Jerusalem, the Temple Mount (Arabic: Haram al-Sharif, or Noble Sanctuary) offers a special case. In June 1967, Israeli defense minister Moshe Dayan wisely opted to maintain the prior status quo on the Mount—autonomous religious rule over the two holy mosques by Muslim authorities and no Jewish prayer on the Mount—with the addition of the right of Israeli Jews to visit the Mount. The Jewish right to pray at the Western Wall of the Mount in the newly conquered Jewish Quarter was not up for negotiation with the conquered Arab authorities. At that time, prevailing rabbinical rulings in any case prohibited observant Jews from ascending the Mount, lest they find themselves physically above the long-buried holy of holies, the ruins of two successive sacred Jewish temples. The mosques on the Mount represent the third-holiest site of Islam, after Mecca and Medina, and are of far-reaching significance to more than 1 billion Muslims throughout the world.

But in the course of nearly fifty years of occupation, nationalist extremist Jews have concluded that there are areas on the Mount where they can pray and have proceeded to try to do so in the face of widespread objections from Palestinian Muslims and the Jordanian monarchy, which bears special treaty-bound responsibility, both fearing an attempt by fanatic Jews to destroy the mosques and rebuild the Temple. In 2014, and particularly in late 2015, this dynamic led to considerable violence in Jerusalem and tension on and around the Mount, which remains a primary focus of a possible new conflagration that would have heavy Muslim-Jewish religious ramifications of near global proportions.

In Israeli-Palestinian final-status negotiations such as those held in 2013 and 2014, the PLO has generally agreed to negotiate the fate of greater Jerusalem and its Jewish population as a separate issue. Recent years have witnessed a major push by Israeli governments—left, center, and right—to complete a circle of Jewish neighborhoods surrounding Arab East Jerusalem and to expand Jewish settlement in the biblical City of David near the Old City, where major ancient Hebrew archeological remains have been unearthed. These Jerusalem settlement activities are designed to cement Israeli control over the expanded city and render it geographically difficult for a West Bank–based Palestinian state to maintain a capital in Arab East Jerusalem that is territorially contiguous with the state itself.

SETTLEMENT RATIONALES: HERITAGE, IDEOLOGY, LOW-QUALITY HOUSING, SECURITY

These historical aspects and legal distinctions are significant in seeking an understanding of the rationale or rationales for the settlements.

The early settlements at the Etzion Bloc and Hebron, as well as within Arab East Jerusalem, had a "heritage" rationale: righting perceived wrongs from 1948 and earlier that have become part of Israeli folklore.

Religious Zionist ideology inspired the Gush Emunim (Bloc of Believers) settlements in the West Bank mountain heartland that began in 1976

and 1977. The settlers sought to resurrect biblical Hebrew sites of religious-ideological significance. Construction of settlements at or near these
sites reflected the dual argument that Zionism had to aspire to return to
these very regions despite their large Palestinian Arab populations and
that the act of return and resettlement would help usher in a new messianist age. Note that around 15 percent of the settlers are American Jewish
immigrants, mostly religious Zionists, who tend to add a very American
"manifest destiny" outlook to their Jewish religiosity.

Religious idealists established most of the West Bank's so-called unau-
thorized outposts—which, unlike the settlements, were never officially
sponsored or approved by state institutions—at times using highly dubi-
ous means such as forged deeds and squatting rights, all under the protective eye of the IDF occupying army, to confiscate private Palestinian
lands. Such outpost activity has in recent years been intended to skirt
restrictions on establishing new settlements imposed by Israeli leaders in
deference to international pressure and protests from moderate members
of governing coalitions.

The "hilltop youth" and the Third Temple movement are small minority spin-offs of this messianist mind-set. The former are second- and
third-generation settlers engaged in provocative and "price tag" attacks
against Palestinian residents, mosques, and Christian institutions, with
the term "price tag" referring to a deterrent attack launched by settlers in
response to perceived Arab offenses that are themselves responses to
hostile settler behavior. At its most extreme, the price tag movement
advocates burning of churches and mosques, murder of Arabs, and establishment of a "State of Judea" in the West Bank. While the movement
appears to comprise only a handful of youthful Israeli misfits, they have
successfully evaded arrest and prosecution and are capable of igniting
major friction and unrest. Perhaps most distressingly, the mainstream
ideological settler movement appears to be incapable of owning up to its
responsibility for spawning and reining in such extremist spin-offs.

The Third Temple activists, also a small minority, believe that Israel
cannot wait for a messiah in order to rebuild Solomon's Temple on the
Temple Mount. Accordingly, they seek to remove the mosques on the
Mount in order to accelerate their agenda.

While the Israeli establishment has largely come to terms with the
broader religious settler movement and, indeed, been partly taken over
by it (see below), these more extreme fringe organizations have generally
encountered a sharp response from security authorities, who fear the
potential explosive effect of their acts not only on the Israeli-Palestinian
conflict but also on Muslim-Jewish relations on a much broader scale.
Yet, broadly speaking, efforts by Israeli law enforcement institutions to
suppress blatant criminal activity by settlers and to apprehend perpetrators have been less than comprehensive.

A large proportion of the West Bank settlers, those not strongly driven ideologically, were at least originally motivated by a desire to improve their quality of life by taking advantage of heavy government housing subsidies and incentives and virtually cost-free plots of land. These settlers are particularly concentrated in settlement "blocs" that abut the pre-1967 green line boundary between the West Bank and Israel; many commute to work in cities inside Israel proper. These blocs, where roughly 75 percent of the settlers live, are frequently mentioned in two-state-solution discussions regarding agreed alterations to the green line boundary. Note that left-oriented Israeli governments, as well as those dominated by the right wing, have offered subsidies and incentives to settle near the green line and in the Jordan Valley.

Finally, the state initiated some settlements with security considerations in mind. The Jordan Valley is the best example: settlement there was designed to ensure a permanent Israeli presence on a strategic strip of land separating the West Bank from (East Bank) Jordan, thereby ostensibly preventing hostile infiltration in the short term and avoiding demographic contiguity between West Bank Palestinians and possibly hostile Palestinians to Israel's east in the long term. Ariel Sharon, who for decades dominated West Bank and Gaza settlement planning, also saw the mountain heartland settlements as guaranteeing Israel access to key strategic high ground in times of war with Arab states to the east or even Iran. Sharon also engineered the Gaza Strip settlements, using settlement blocs comprising a few thousand settlers, to disrupt the continuity of Palestinian cities and towns populated by more than (in 2005) 1.5 million Arabs.

Notably, the Jordan Valley as a security boundary played a key role in undermining the abortive two-state negotiations spearheaded in 2013 and 2014 by US Secretary of State John Kerry (see chapter 7). And the Israeli right wing and some security authorities cite the West Bank heartland settlements as Israel's guarantee against territorial concessions that would allow hostile Palestinians to fire rockets at Israeli cities from the very close range of the West Bank.

THE POLITICS OF SETTLEMENT

Broadly speaking, Likud-led right-wing governments have, since 1977, spearheaded the settlement project, while Labor-led governments have sought to limit settlement to greater Jerusalem, the Jordan Valley, and the settlement blocs. But the West Bank settlement project began after 1967 under Labor, and while Labor governments have taken a more proactive approach to peace with the Palestinians and to consequent withdrawal from part or all of the territories, they have also, for political and ideological reasons, generally tolerated the settler movement and repeatedly ac-

quiesced in the faits accomplis created by the dynamic messianist settlers
in the West Bank. The Ehud Barak government of 1999 and 2000, for
example, witnessed record rates of settlement, presumably because then
prime minister Barak hoped to ensure right-wing passivity while he proceeded with dynamic peace processes with the PLO and Syria.

Still, Labor tended to favor settlement blocs with a Jewish majority
and close access to Israel proper. In contrast, most of the Israeli Right's
settlement approach has involved interspersing settlements in the midst
of heavy Arab population concentrations. In 1994 Ariel Sharon, who
spearheaded the settlement drive, described this to me graphically as
placing a settlement on a hilltop between two valleys populated by Arabs, with the goal of keeping them from joining forces, and multiplying
this tactic throughout the West Bank and even Gaza. The first policy
favors separation; the second deliberately complicates it.

Interestingly, Sharon—the very same politician who had earlier shepherded the West Bank and Gaza settlement project to ongoing expansion—ultimately provided the only instance of large-scale dismantling of
West Bank and Gaza settlements recorded thus far. Note that Sharon also
took charge of removing the Sinai settlements as a condition for peace
with Egypt in the late 1970s. He was in many ways the ultimate cynical
pragmatist, but one devoid of deep strategic understanding.

Thus, Sharon did not remove all the settlements from the Gaza Strip
and four settlements from the northern West Bank because he believed in
peace and a two-state solution in 2005—he was almost certainly a total
skeptic in this regard. Rather, he did so as the minimal territorial concession he thought at the time would rebuff American, international, and
internal Israeli pressure to avoid the slippery slope of a one-state solution
that increasingly appears to be the consequence of unlimited settlement
spread. His record in having presided over the IDF's brutal suppression
of the second intifada, beginning in 2002, gave him the popular credibility needed by any Israeli leader contemplating the dismantling of settlements, whatever the reason.

When he fell ill and left office shortly after the Gaza disengagement,
Sharon was apparently contemplating additional West Bank military and
settlement withdrawals. Since then, repeated large-scale aggression
against Israeli civilians by the Hamas Islamist movement that took control of the Gaza Strip in a bloody coup in 2007 has had the effect in
mainstream Israeli circles of discrediting a similar unilateral withdrawal
and dismantling of settlements by Israel on the West Bank.

The Netanyahu governments of the years beginning in 2009 have
comprised significant pro-settler components and facilitated settlement
spread, while Netanyahu himself has ostensibly been committed to a
two-state solution and to cooperating with US-led two-state initiatives.
Repeated instances of Palestinian terrorism against Israeli civilians and,
in recent years, the sharp deterioration of the entire Arab state system

surrounding Israel—including the fragmenting of the Palestinian polity between the West Bank/Fatah and Gaza/Hamas—have significantly strengthened the inclination of a large majority of Israelis to tolerate the settlements in view of the seeming absence of a viable political alternative.

For years, Netanyahu has proven adept at raising and lowering the flame under the settlement project as a tool for leveraging his relationship with both the international community and his own right-wing constituency. Thus, in the course of US-led peace efforts between 2010 and 2014, he conveniently played ignorant of settlement starts that constituted an affront to the United States but rallied the prime minister's supporters. In contrast, in 2015 he quietly froze construction starts to placate the European Union and thereby weaken its economic-sanctions threat and to strengthen his bargaining position as he sought to rebuff international condemnation of draconian security measures invoked against Palestinian violence that began over the Temple Mount issue. Yet in May 2015 Netanyahu could allow himself to form a government that offered no more than an anodyne pledge to "advance the diplomatic process and . . . strive for a peace agreement with the Palestinians and with all of our neighbors."

The most significant settler-related political development of recent years has been the success of the ideological settler movement in entering the political and security mainstream and establishing itself as a "new elite" in Israeli society. The settler leadership long understood that to succeed in the long run, this messianist movement, the most dynamic element on the Israeli scene, eventually had to "settle in the hearts and minds of the Israeli mainstream." After the removal of a mere sixteen hundred settler families from the Gaza Strip in 2005, entering the national leadership became an urgent mission in order to prevent such a large-scale evacuation in the West Bank.

By 2015, settlers or their sympathizers were increasingly evident in the ruling Likud party and in parties to its ideological right, in the financial institutions responsible for expanding and subsidizing the settlement movement, and among the heads of the security establishment that could conceivably be called upon one day to remove West Bank settlements in accordance with Israeli-Palestinian peace accords. While the settlers have never achieved anything approaching party-political dominance, and while most Israelis have never visited a settlement and are still prepared to discuss removing settlements to facilitate peace, the ideological settlers have excelled at exploiting the bureaucracy (which is far more permanent than specific ministers or military commanders) and exploiting legal grey areas with great sophistication.

They have entered the security community en mass. If, in 1990, only 2.5 percent of infantry officer cadets in the IDF were religious nationalist, by 2011 that figure had climbed dramatically to 42 percent. In 2011, an

Orthodox Jew became head of the Shin Bet, Israel's internal security arm, the first to head one of the main branches of the Israeli security establishment. In 2015 his deputy, an Orthodox Jew who had once lived in a settlement with extremist connections, was appointed chief of the Israel Police with virtually no public objections raised regarding his background.

And the settlers are adept at public relations. At the City of David (Silwan) in East Jerusalem, for example, where a settler enterprise has engaged in extensive archeological exploration and restoration, public funds are used to bring high school students and soldiers to visit, hear lectures, and in effect support the settlers' drive for further recognition and funds.

All these dynamic activities take place while Israel's relatively indifferent majority sits by. This phenomenon must give us pause: Wasn't Israel established by a largely secular nationalist Zionist movement bent on abandoning Diaspora religiosity and passivity, creating a new Jew who works and defends the land where Judaism was born, and dealing pragmatically—not in a messianist context—with Israel's neighbors? Was it only the 1967 war with its conquest of the West Bank biblical heartland (and its large Palestinian population) that plunged Israel into the folly of large-scale settlement with its quasi-colonialist ills?

Prominent American political theorist Michael Walzer posits in a recent book that the desecularization of Zionism may be an inevitable development. Indian and Algerian independence was also achieved by secular nationalists, then, beginning about thirty years later, gradually taken over by religious nationalist revivals. He describes this religious pull as an "undertow" or "dark face" nurtured all along, in Israel's case, by a kind of secular Zionist messianism that never really dispensed with religious motifs and values. Note, for example, that the quintessential Zionist concept of *aliyah*, or ascendance to settle the land, borrows directly from Jewish prayer ritual—ascending to the *bama* to read the Torah. Significantly, Walzer notes, Palestinian nationalism began as a secular Arab response to Zionism and is gradually, with the rise to power of Hamas, becoming religious fundamentalist.

By 2015, in view of the absence of a viable Arab-Israel peace process and the chaos visiting the surrounding Arab world, the increasingly influential settler establishment and its supporters appeared confident that Israel's grip on the territories was not about to be challenged. With the passage of the years after 1967 and particularly after the rise to power of right-wing governments from 1977 on, the messianist settler movement and the almost mystical pull exercised on its imagination by the soil of Judea and Samaria have nourished one another.

The movement, spearheaded by Gush Emunim, drew on the teachings of Rabbi Abraham Isaac Kook and his son, Zvi Yehuda. The elder Kook viewed the Zionist project as the dawning of redemption; the younger taught that the 1967 Six-Day War was the miraculous proof. Accordingly, the religious nationalist movement believed that settling the land of the West Bank would usher in the messiah, whereas withdrawing from the land would invite divine punishment. Note that these teachings constituted for religious Jews a sharp departure from Diaspora rejection of Zionism as a violation of God's will and an attempt to force redemption and that ultra-Orthodox Jews, in both Israel and the Diaspora, continue, to one extent or another, to reject Zionism on this basis.

Beginning in 2005, it took the Sharon government and its successors ten years and roughly $2 billion to remove and relocate a mere eight thousand settlers from the Gaza Strip. Even if we assume for a moment that a strong, peace-minded, and charismatic Palestinian leader offers tomorrow to implement a two-state solution along terms roughly acceptable to close to two-thirds of Israeli Jews and the entire Arab world and international community, the required removal of between eighty and one hundred thousand settlers from isolated West Bank settlements—those settlements lying beyond the green line blocs that are candidates for land "swaps" with the Palestinians—seems increasingly unrealistic from a domestic Israeli political standpoint in terms of both governmental decision making and security force implementation.

POLITICS AND ASSASSINATION

A second turning point in Israeli attitudes since 1967 was the assassination in November 1995 of Prime Minister Yitzhak Rabin by a religious nationalist settlements supporter. The assassin, Yigal Amir, had been deeply influenced and incited by ultranationalist rabbis who opposed Rabin's peace policies with the Palestinians on the grounds that they were compromising sacred territories in the West Bank and thereby endangering the future of the Jewish state and the Jewish people. The deterrent effect of this assassination on subsequent Israeli leaders is impossible to measure. Prime Minister Netanyahu did agree in 1996 and 1997 to a territorial compromise within the city of Hebron, and Ariel Sharon presided over the withdrawal from the entirety of the Gaza Strip in 2005. But these were relatively marginal events: Netanyahu did not give up Jewish control of Hebron's holy sites, and the Gaza Strip is generally not considered part of the biblical Land of Israel—hence not sacred. Moreover, Israeli leaders have been far better protected from harm since Rabin's death. Yet there can be no doubt that even a dovish leader like Ehud Olmert in 2008 paused when contemplating the practical personal consequences of the territorial deal, including a Palestinian capital and internationally administered holy sites in the heart of Jerusalem, that he offered Palestinian leader Mahmoud Abbas (and that Abbas rejected; see chapters 6 and 7).

Today—indeed, for several decades—the Israeli political scene can be increasingly characterized as follows: On the one hand, a dynamic and messianist right wing has grasped enough political power to ensure the ongoing expansion of the settlement enterprise in the West Bank and East Jerusalem. It is either so suspicious or so racially disdainful of Palestinians that it seeks to incorporate them and their homes into a single state or a quasi-Bantustan in which Palestinians are granted second-class citizenship in the guise of "autonomy" (see chapter 9).

On the other hand, a shrinking Zionist liberal wing is incapable not only of stopping the settlements but also—though it seems unable to admit it—of meeting minimal Palestinian terms for a two-state solution, not to mention compelling tens of thousands of settlers to abandon their homes in favor of peace. Its ideas for a two-state solution have failed. A majority of Israelis perceive this group as naively wanting peace for the sake of peace and cultivating a false sense of Israeli "guilt" regarding the occupation and the absence of a resolution, while ignoring Israel's genuine security interests.

Between the Right and the Left is a fluid political Center that either has more or less given up on peace with the Palestinians and prefers to concentrate on quality-of-life issues or wants Israel to save itself from demographic disaster by somehow withdrawing from heavily populated West Bank territories. It can explain neither how it will remove one hundred thousand settlers who live beyond the settlement blocs and security fence nor how it will prevent Hamas and other terrorists from using the West Bank as a launching pad to attack Israel—unless it leaves the IDF in place in the West Bank, in which case it has not ended the occupation (see chapter 8).

The political Right is increasingly nationalistic, boasting patriotic fervor and playing on irrationally inflated "the world is against us" fears. It trumpets threats (e.g., by the Iranian, Hizballah, and Hamas leaderships) of existential destruction; plays up Holocaust memories to generate fear of compromise even with relatively moderate Palestinians, whose belief system (see chapter 5) can easily be shown to comprise views incompatible with those of most Israelis and can therefore be labeled "incitement"; cultivates jingoistic legislative initiatives about "loyalty oaths," a "Jewish nation state," and the need for domestic primacy of Hebrew over Arabic; and sponsors education increasingly emphasizing fundamentalist Jewish religious tenets rather than the founding fathers' secular Zionist values. Its growing control over what were once left-leaning media outlets, state and privately owned, facilitates this dynamic. Over the past twenty-five years, it has been able to draw on the support of a large majority of the million-plus Jews and their relatives who immigrated from the former Soviet Union and brought with them hawkish views about territorial compromise and quasi-racist views of Arabs.

In contrast, the only representatives of the Left seemingly still capable of being elected to lead the country are "security doves" like Yitzhak Rabin and Ehud Barak who package a two-state solution not as diplomacy and peace but as enhanced security for Israel wrapped in deep skepticism about Palestinian capabilities. The only leader to abandon territories in the past fifteen years was Ariel Sharon, who exploited his own hawkish image to pull Israel out of the Gaza Strip and a portion of the northern West Bank in 2005. The disastrous aftermath of that withdrawal—Palestinian failure to make good on a golden opportunity for state-building, followed by a Hamas takeover in Gaza and repeated wars between Hamas and Israel—has in any case discredited the move in the eyes of many of its original supporters.

At a deeper, pre-1967 societal level, the absence of a basic consensus and sense of purpose can be traced to a number of trends and dynamics that were distorted and neglected from the start in 1948. Seemingly easy to ignore for years, these have lately risen to the surface, exacerbated by the internal Israeli divide over the fate of the Palestinian issue.

One is education. Separate tracks for educating secular, religious nationalist, ultra-Orthodox, and Arab youth mean that many Israelis grow up apart from one another and not necessarily sharing common values. As long as the secular track was dominant among the Jewish population and the Arab track (actually fragmented among Muslim, Christian, and Druze youth) was the domain of an essentially nonparticipatory segment of the country, the effect was to minimize the alienating effects of the 1948 decision not to amalgamate the ethnic and religious education tracks that prevailed under the British Mandate in favor of a national education curriculum.

Today, in contrast, the effects are huge. First-grade students from the ultra-Orthodox and Arab sectors—the former non-Zionist, the latter anti-Zionist—constitute a majority of all first-grade students in the country. Many of the ultra-Orthodox schools offer almost nothing of the core curriculum of mathematics, English, history, and civics. In June 2015, President Reuven Rivlin told secular and religious nationalist Israelis pointedly that they could no longer look upon Israeli Arabs and ultra-Orthodox in terms of "majority and minority." Rather, in view of demographic forecasts, they should start thinking of "four tribes," roughly equal in size: national-secular, national-Orthodox, Arab, and ultra-Orthodox ("Haredi"). As if a tribal national division offers a helpful way to build national unity, and as if the increasingly tribal nature of the chaos in the Arab world surrounding Israel offers a helpful model for nation building.

Among the Zionist "half" of Israelis, while secular Jews still vastly outnumber religious nationalists, the latter not only constitute the backbone of the messianist settler movement but also have, as noted earlier, exploited their political clout and galvanized their strong sense of purpose to guide the graduates of their education system increasingly to political leadership and command positions in the security community.

Does this mean that the vaunted Israeli "people's army" is becoming an arm of fundamentalist Judaism, serving the messianist values that the religious nationalist movement inculcates in its schools and yeshivas? Not necessarily—or at least not yet. Most religious Jews in Israel are generally just as attuned to Israeli democracy as are the secular; in recent years, they just seem more adept at exploiting it for their purposes. When the IDF was sent to evacuate the Gaza Strip settlements in 2005, there was almost no refusal to obey orders on the part of religious officers. Still, a constant drive to control all or significant parts of the Ministry of Education reflects the religious nationalist emphasis on educating secular youth based on religious values. In 2014, for example, the secular high school system devoted ten times as many resources to education for traditionalist, Orthodox-defined "Jewish values" as for "democratic values" promoted by secular liberals. Over time, and even allowing for push-back by parents of non-Orthodox youth, these dynamics will almost certainly affect Israeli democracy by militating against pluralism and tolerance.

Paradoxically, the secular political sector in Israel led a campaign in 2013 to conscript ultra-Orthodox youth and remove the blanket exemption from service granted them by Prime Minister David Ben Gurion in the early 1950s. Back then, Ben Gurion allegedly yielded to the dictum of the Hazon Ish, a distinguished ultra-Orthodox rabbi, that secular Jews' "empty wagon" had to make way on a figurative bridge for religious Jews' "full wagon." The prime minister was also at the time apparently moved to help preserve the tiny remnant of ultra-Orthodoxy, representing the Judaism dominant in eastern Europe a mere generation or two earlier, that had survived the Holocaust. Of course, at the time both Orthodox and ultra-Orthodox Jews formed relatively small minorities bereft of political influence.

But as religious nationalist Jews have moved into the mainstream and the ultra-Orthodox minority has grown, the secular and religious nationalist sectors have pressured to force ultra-Orthodox conscription in the name of national unity based on universal burden sharing. Unless a future government dependent on ultra-Orthodox votes restores the exemption (in 2015 that seemed quite likely), military service for ultra-Orthodox men will presumably accomplish what the secular and Orthodox sectors intend: channel many of them into the mainstream of productive work and work-related education rather than strictly religious studies that guarantee a life of poverty and nonproductivity and in turn—even if one believes that a lifetime of prayer adds a vital existential dimension to Jewish life—constitute a huge drag on a modern economy.

In other words secular Israel has, in the name of greater long-term socioeconomic integration, willingly created a new reality whereby religious influence in the IDF is augmented still further. This probably means more rabbinical influence over military decision making, attempts to isolate female soldiers from contact with males, and additional antidemocratic and messianist measures.

One additional fragmenting and frightening aspect of education bears mention in the context of societal divisions. In June 2015, the Bank of Israel predicted that the lack of integration of Israel's growing Arab and ultra-Orthodox sectors into the more sophisticated echelons of the workforce—the former due to prejudice, the latter by choice, and both due to inadequate education—would within several decades bankrupt the Israeli economy.

Clearly, in looking at the Israeli security community and Israeli politics, and even allowing for the near universality of at least a modicum of democratic values, the religious nationalists, with their concept of settling the West Bank as messianist redemption regardless of the demographic and political consequences, emerge as a rising elite to be reckoned with. That the Jewish Home party, which champions these beliefs and espouses essentially an apartheid concept for the West Bank, could claim a potential electorate in early 2015, fully half of which comprises secular youths inspired by the party leadership's trumpeting of Jewish identity and "values," reinforces the impression that a new elite is on the rise.

Further, before leaving the issue of Israeli democracy, we cannot but take notice of polls that indicate a high percentage of Israelis who, when confronted by the hypothetical need to choose, prefer the concept of a Jewish state over the concept of a democratic one—a persuasion that would render it easier for an Israeli government to seek to permanently control the West Bank without fully enfranchising its Arab population. An equally high percentage is prepared to consider a variety of effectively nondemocratic measures, such as marginalizing the Arabic language and preventing Arabs from living in Jewish towns and villages, in dealing with the Israeli Arab community.

This should not surprise us if we recall that, according to the Israel Democracy Institute, 80 percent of Israeli Jews believe in God, and 70 percent believe the Jews are a chosen people. It is generally accepted among Western democracies that religious adherence tends to coincide with political conservatism. Then, too, observant Judaism, unlike Christianity but like Islam, is an all-encompassing set of beliefs that involve politics and geography. Add to this the rise of militant Islam among Israel's neighbors, and the Arab-Israel conflict is increasingly taking on attributes of a Jewish-Muslim confrontation rather than a national conflict.

This could have far-reaching implications. National conflicts are relatively easy to contain and, if not resolve, then at least manage. In contrast, a religious conflict easily spreads beyond national borders and perpetuates itself, often with apocalyptic, all-or-nothing implications.

IS THE HOLOCAUST A DIVISIVE FACTOR?

Apropos apocalyptic issues, and before we move on from the divisive issues that play a role in Israeli Jewish disunity, a word is in order regarding the Holocaust. It is at times a divisive element in the Israeli discourse but should not be exaggerated in the Israeli, as opposed to the global Jewish, context.

In contemporary Israel, right-wing leaders like Netanyahu tend to use Holocaust references as a means of illustrating and even aggrandizing the severity of threats to Israel's security. The comparisons are facilitated by the fact that Israel's Islamist enemies, from Iran via Hizballah to the Islamic State and Hamas, embrace extreme anti-Semitic beliefs and myths, frequently deny the Holocaust, and threaten regularly to destroy Israel and occasionally to destroy the world's Jews.

Holocaust references are particularly convenient for hawks who prefer to avoid dealing with pragmatic ideas for compromise or conciliation put forward by others on the political and even security spectrum. After all, they ostensibly obviate the need for rational debate. If Hizballah leader Hassan Nasrallah is "Hitler," the conversation about Israel's relationship with southern Lebanon's Shiites is over. If Hamas embraces *The Protocols of the Elders of Zion* (a notorious anti-Semitic forgery), why should we discuss with it humanitarian aid for Gazans or a cease-fire or a prisoner exchange? If President Barack Obama's concessions to Iran in the course of the nuclear negotiations that culminated in July 2015 in agreement can be compared to Neville Chamberlain's historic capitulation at Munich, the discussion is ostensibly over. When, in the Netanyahu government that served prior to March 2013, the minister of education (not a Likudnik but an Orthodox Jew) insisted on introducing Holocaust education at the nursery school level in Israel, the government's critics understood this as a means of instilling unjustified existential fears in the minds of children totally lacking rational intellectual filters.

The Holocaust figures liberally in Arab narratives concerning the creation of the state of Israel. This, too, is convenient: Germans killed Jews, and we Palestinians have to bear the burden. In a vastly different context, some Israeli observers understand the Holocaust to constitute a more central factor in the Jewish identity of many Diaspora communities, including the American, than in Israeli identity. Moreover, many Israelis, secular and religious, on the right and on the left, understand the narrative according to which the Holocaust is the primary reason for the creation of Israel, whether voiced by Arabs, Jews, or others, as an anti-Zionist attempt to downplay Israel as the historic national homeland of the Jewish people and to ignore the country's roots in the fifty years of Zionist endeavor that preceded World War II.

Having noted all these aspects of Holocaust culture in Israel, it would be incorrect to state that this is a primary divisive factor in the way the country addresses the Palestinian issue.

ISRAEL'S ARAB CITIZENS

Israel's occupation of several million Palestinian noncitizens began in 1967 and went on to generate what became known as the Palestinian issue and the proposed two-state solution. Prior to then, as we shall see in chapter 6, between 1948 and 1967 two Arab states, Jordan and Egypt, had occupied the West Bank, East Jerusalem, and the Gaza Strip, and for better or for worse the only aspect of the Palestinian problem that engaged the world was the refugee issue—and even that was not laid provocatively at Israel's doorstep. Indeed, prior to 1967 Israel repatriated tens of thousands of Palestinian refugees through a family-reunification program that took much of the sting out of the relatively minor (by today's standards) complaints it confronted over the Palestinians in the aftermath of the 1948 war.

After 1967, not only would Israel's military occupation of the Palestinian territories gradually become a major factor in the way the international community looked at the Middle East, but the occupation, and particularly the failure of the two sides after 1993 to negotiate the creation of a Palestinian state, would also radicalize the leadership of the Israeli Arab community.

That the intellectual and political leaders of the Israeli Arab community increasingly insist on being called "Palestinian citizens of Israel" and not "Israeli Arabs" offers a semantic hint as to its national self-image as it has emerged since 1967. Prior to 1966, we recall, Israeli Arabs lived under highly restrictive military government. They were also, incidentally, generally disparaged by those Palestinians who in 1948 had been dispersed throughout the Arab world: the Israeli Arabs had somehow transgressed national values by remaining in Israel and not fleeing or being expelled during the events of 1948.

The 1967 war, with its Israeli conquest of the West Bank, East Jerusalem, and the Gaza Strip, effectively restored contact between Israel's Palestinian population and that of the rest of Palestine and, through it, with the Palestinian diaspora in the Arab world and beyond. In the mistaken belief that open borders and commerce would ensure Israeli-Palestinian tranquility and Palestinian economic well-being and reduce or prevent Palestinian hostility toward Israeli military rule, then minister of defense Moshe Dayan in June 1967 threw open the Israel–West Bank and Israel–Gaza green line boundaries to free movement. Those boundaries have since been largely closed to passage by Israeli Jews, but the West Bank remains open to Arab citizens of Israel in deference to the close relation-

ship between the two Palestinian populations while ignoring the consequences for Israeli Arab ideology.

True, the reintegration of the Palestinian citizens of Israel into the
Palestinian mainstream has here and there furthered the cause of Israeli-
Palestinian peace—for instance, when Arab member of Knesset Ahmed
Tibi served occasionally as a go-between, connecting and advising the
Israeli and PLO leaderships. But for the most part it has inspired the
Palestinian intellectual and political elite of Israel to adopt positions re-
garding the nature of the state of Israel that are more extreme even than
those of the West Bank–based PLO leadership.

Fatah/PLO leaders have blatantly refused in recent years to recognize
Israel as a Jewish state (although Yasser Arafat did so in the forgotten
past, in 1988 in the Algiers declaration) or the nation-state of the Jewish
people, even if adequate protection and equal citizenship status are en-
sured for its Arab minority. Rhetorically, they leave it to Israel to "define
itself as it likes," while insisting their own future state be understood as
the state of the Palestinian people and, like all Arab states except Lebanon, defined as Arab and relying on traditional Islamic law (Sharia). As
we shall see in chapter 6, this reflects their continual insistence, and that
of virtually all Arabs and many Muslims, that the Jews are not a people
and do not have national roots in the Holy Land. It also almost certainly
reflects the PLO leadership's belief that a two-state solution in which
Palestine belongs to Palestinian Arabs while Israel is not recognized as
belonging to the Jewish people leaves the historical door open for the
gradual "Palestinization" of Israel by dint of a high Palestinian birth rate,
refugee return, and overall attrition of the Israeli Jewish population.

Still, the PLO does not pretend to "define" Israel's sovereign nature
through the instrument of a treaty creating a Palestinian state alongside
Israel. Enter the Israeli Arab community. Inspired first by the post-1993
Oslo peace process and its promise of Palestinian national self-determination, then by the virtual demise of that process and the gradual realization that a Palestinian state next door is not a likely near-term eventual-
ity, the Israeli Arab elite published in 2006 and 2007 a series of "vision"
documents that defined its view of what Israel was and what it should
be—a view that Israeli Jews, not surprisingly, found extreme.

Essentially, the Israeli Arab "vision" rejects Israel's legitimacy as a
Jewish state, defines it as a colonial creation, and demands that it adopt
a binational (i.e., not Jewish Zionist) identity that places its Palestinian
Arab population on a completely equal national status with Jews. In re-
verting to 1948 issues—that is, reraising the question of Israel's existence
as a Jewish state—to frame Israeli Arab attitudes toward Israel, these
documents demand that Israel cancel the law of return (for Jews) and
recognize the right of return (for Arabs who left in 1948 and their descendants).

Notably, the Israeli-Arab rank and file is to all appearances far less ideological than its leaders. Many polls indicate that most Arab citizens of Israel aspire primarily to a better material life and a higher degree of socioeconomic parity with Jews and are prepared to live as equal citizens in a "Jewish state." Certainly they have in recent years begun to achieve a much improved standard of living as they play prominent roles in important sectors of the Israeli economy. Yet, at election time, these same Arab citizens repeatedly endorse varieties of an extreme political program. Then there are the several hundred thousand Bedouin in the Negev. Broadly impoverished and locked with the government in endless land conflicts of the nomadic herder versus sedentary farmer and urbanite variety, they are, in their frustration, becoming increasingly Islamized. Note, incidentally, that only one-fifth of Israelis are Arab, but three key areas of the country are 50 percent Arab, or nearly so: the Galilee, the Negev, and Jerusalem.

CONCLUSION

In conclusion, it bears emphasis that Israel has always been highly pluralistic and that it is far more democratic today than it was, say, fifty years ago. Further, the Israeli public debate, overshadowed always by the Holocaust and reflecting a constant awareness of the genuine strategic dangers surrounding the country, has often comprised a somewhat paranoid doomsday element (the notorious Jewish *gevald* syndrome) of imminent destruction that, miraculously, never comes to fruition. It is important to keep this in mind when we look at scenarios for Israel's future in a world without an agreed solution to the Palestinian issue.

However, the history of Hebrew sovereignty in the Holy Land in ancient biblical times points to a fairly limited life span—roughly one hundred years—for what we would today call "Jewish states," whether in a unified kingdom or in separate Judaean, Samarian, and Hasmonean entities. Sometimes conquest by stronger powers was the limiting factor; at other times, internal tension and conflict of the sort we have described here led to state collapse or conquest. As Israel approaches age seventy, that is food for thought.

FOUR

The Global Jewish Factor

The Diaspora, Anti-Semitism

The American Jewish community, which constitutes nearly half of world Jewry, was instrumental in Israel's founding and has helped support it financially and politically ever since. Its influence in the halls of power in Washington has been critical for Israel, which, by most standards of identity measurement, has overtaken American Jewry as the world's largest Jewish community and has increasingly given the latter a focus of group identity. If Israel enjoys a special relationship with Washington, based on security and values, the American Jewish community deserves a major part of the credit.

The reciprocal interaction over the decades among Israel, the United States, and American Jewry led me back in the mid-1990s to term the relationship a "strategic triangle." For decades, the grand strategy of close and positive interaction with Washington and the American Jewish community has served Israel's overall security and well-being. Yet today there are signs of growing imbalance that lead us to ask whether the ongoing and seemingly unresolvable Palestinian conflict, with its dimensions of occupation, creeping annexation, and extremist Jewish behavior, poses a threat to the viability of this triangle. And if so, what does this mean for Israel and, for that matter, for American Jews?

All three sides of the triangle are changing in ways that affect the trilateral relationship. The United States is groping to comprehend the Middle East and reassess its interests there. In the post-9/11 era, successive administrations have made one error after another in the region: invading Iraq, misapplying principles of democratization and failing in this enterprise, tolerating Islamist extremist Iran and its hostile behavior in exchange for a temporary solution to its nuclear project, misreading the "Arab Spring," and encouraging putatively "moderate" Islamism to the detriment of US allies. As we shall see in chapter 7, Washington has also badly overestimated its capacity to "solve" the Israeli-Palestinian conflict.

American politics are also changing, with ethnic minorities—Hispanic, African American, Asian American—predicted eventually to constitute a demographic majority. This, combined with the growing influence of religious politics within the traditional white majority, appears to some in Israel—who assume that American Jews behave like the white majority and who are ignorant of the American Jewish mainstream's liberal legacy—to pose new but as yet nebulous challenges to American Jewish influence at the national level regarding Israel.

At the same time, the American Jewish community itself is changing radically. American Judaism is a thoroughly mainstream religion in a non-Jewish country. The challenges of assimilation and intermarriage seem to a secular Israeli observer almost to be generating a new American-style religion among the Conservative and Reform Jewish communities and among nonaffiliated and secular Jews. That emerging religious stream places a high priority on embracing common denominators with other religions while continuing to advocate liberal values (Palestinian national rights, civil liberties in Israel) that are increasingly at odds with the direction in which the Israeli mainstream is moving and seem, to many Israeli eyes, increasingly detached from Middle East realities. Extensive conversion to Judaism is bringing vibrant non-Jewish values into the mix. To the extent that American Jews see the Israeli-Palestinian conflict as centering on the issue of human and minority rights, they are out of step with most Israelis, who increasingly understand the conflict as tribal, religious, and existential. Nor does the vast majority of American Jews make voting decisions based on the status of United States–Israel relations, even if many profess to "care about Israel." This helps explain the growing perceptual gap between American liberals and Israeli secular progressives.

Meanwhile, as the mainstream slowly becomes more alienated, American Jewry's Orthodox minority, whose value system clashes less with that of contemporary Israel, is growing in numbers and influence. Its contribution in coin and personnel to the West Bank settler movement should not be underestimated, just as the contribution of American Jewish ultra-Orthodoxy to the powerful and increasingly right-wing Israeli ultra-Orthodox sector is considerable. Israeli leaders like Likud's Benjamin Netanyahu and Jewish Home leader Naftali Bennett, with their strong roots in the American Jewish community, are well aware of this.

If in the past, even when right-wing governments ruled in Jerusalem, Israel's leaders harkened to the urgings and warnings of leaders of the American Jewish liberal mainstream, in recent years they are more responsive to the money and ideology of the likes of gambling mogul Sheldon Adelson, who rejects a two-state solution and told a conference in Washington, DC, on November 9, 2014, "I don't think the Bible says anything about democracy. . . . Israel isn't going to be a democratic state—so what?" Adelson's extreme points of view are associated with Republican and minority Jewish organizations like the Republican Jewish Coalition and the Zionist Organization of America rather than with the American Jewish majority.

The events of February and March 2015 in the Israeli-American relationship pointed to the possibility that Netanyahu was bent on recasting the structure of the institutions that bind Israel and US Jewry. Against the advice of most of Israel's supporters in the American Jewish community, initially including mainstream Jewish advocacy organizations like the American Israel Public Affairs Committee (AIPAC) and the Anti-defamation League (ADL), Netanyahu defied the will of the Barack Obama administration and, with Republican support, insisted on addressing Congress to denounce the administration's emerging nuclear agreement with Iran. He delivered his speech exactly two weeks before national elections in Israel. The upshot was that Israel's own security and politically oriented divide regarding Iran, wherein leading retired security chiefs openly opposed Netanyahu's approach, was superimposed forcefully—along with Israel's electoral politics—on a no less bitter American divide and injected into American Jewish politics.

The American Jewish liberal mainstream has supported Obama and the Iran deal. In broad terms it wants to support Israel but has become increasingly distressed by that country's behavior regarding the Palestinian issue. Now, in early 2015, it confronted an aggressive and unprecedented Israeli challenge to the administration and the Democratic Party regarding Iran. Note that the politics of the American Jewish organizational and advocacy world are anything but democratic and transparent. Veteran communal organizations, whose lay leaders have risen to the top by contributing money, and the professional staffs who run these organizations, often for life and usually with few managerial skills, purport to speak without any substantive mandate in the name of millions of Jews. And generally, on Israel-related issues (unlike, say, liberal issues like women's rights and abortion, which 90 percent of American Jews support at the grassroots national level), American Jews have no other collective communal voice.

These American Jewish leaders have a huge vested organizational interest in the status quo. But they also, for the most part, have a deeply felt understanding of the meaning of an independent Jewish state for the well-being of the Diaspora. So they do not want to rock the boat and will look desperately for ways to reconcile Netanyahu's policies with their own political views and loyalties. Thus, typically, both AIPAC and the ADL ultimately found it politically expedient to support Netanyahu's March 3, 2015, appearance before Congress—where he brought along

Holocaust icon Elie Wiesel to make his point that a deal with Iran is akin to the Munich capitulation of 1938—even though this stand hardly reflected majority American Jewish opinion. By mid-2015, with the unveiling of the Iran nuclear agreement, Netanyahu's ongoing hostility promised yet more heavy tensions within the strategic triangle.

In a similar vein, I recall my own five-year stint representing the American Jewish Committee in Israel and the Middle East. My views on various Israel-related issues were constantly solicited. At the same time, I was pressured to align them with the serving Israeli government, whether under Yitzhak Rabin, Shimon Peres, or Benjamin Netanyahu. Ultimately this schizophrenia obliged me, as a more independent-minded Israeli, to resign.

On a broader scale, countless surveys indicate that erosion of support for Israel is increasingly palpable among the young generation of primarily liberal and Democratic American Jews. Sooner or later this will make itself more strongly felt at the organizational and political levels too, as it becomes increasingly difficult to be both liberal and pro-Israel. As a result, AIPAC's key role in ensuring ongoing US security support for Israel is undoubtedly the most sensitive asset to be guarded by Israel and the American Jewish community alike.

Anti-Semitism is another dimension of the Israel-Diaspora equation that has lately been responding to developments in the Israeli-Palestinian sphere and, in turn, influencing them. This is not the forum for discussing and analyzing the important question of where on the anti-Israel spectrum growing conflict-engendered anti-Israel attitudes in Europe and the United States end and where anti-Semitism begins. Clearly both phenomena are growing, and both should concern Israel and the American Jewish community.

One important difference between them is that anti-Semitism affects Jews in general, regardless of their nationality or politics, whereas anti-Israel opinions may not; indeed, they may at times be voiced by American and European Jews. Another is that, among many Arabs, Iranians, and others in the Muslim world who refuse to accept Jews as a people, and generally unlike in the West, it is increasingly difficult to distinguish between anti-Israel attitudes and anti-Semitism: they are not spread out over a nuanced spectrum as in the West; rather, they are largely one phenomenon that is perhaps symbolized by the repeated graphic representation of Israeli Jews using the most egregious Nazi propaganda stereotypes of Jews. This perforce explains why the remnant of Iran's Jewish community must take great pains to separate itself from Israel in the eyes of the Iranian establishment.

Still, in western Europe, with its growing population of Arabs and other Muslims and its legacy of anti-Semitism among extreme right- and left-wing ideological currents, contemporary trends in public opinion that are fueled by Israel's policies regarding the Palestinian territories are already reducing both popular and institutional support for Israelis as "fellow Europeans." They are even diminishing that vaguely formulated (except in Germany, where it is explicit) post-WWII "historical obligation" to support a Jewish state. In this atmosphere, it is not surprising that growing numbers of European Jews, motivated primarily by fear of militant European Islam, are debating their future in Europe, to the point of considering the possibility of emigrating to Israel and other destinations, even as the European Union adopts tougher policies toward Israel and—pressured by local right-wing reaction—toward Muslim immigration. Still, lest we forget, Europe has numerous other problems—social, economic, security related—that could affect both its attitudes toward Israel and its capacity to make unified decisions regarding the Israeli-Palestinian conflict.

All in all, as the Israeli-Palestinian conflict continues to fester and evade resolution, the alienation of the Israeli right-wing mainstream from the American Jewish Diaspora mainstream will grow. This is almost certain to have a negative effect on support for Israel on the part of the United States. But precisely how and to what extent is difficult to predict. A wide variety of events in the Middle East could exacerbate or moderate it. Nor should the impressive resolve of some American Jewish leaders to hang on to the Israel link and to reconcile all the contradictions at almost any cost be ignored. The Taglit-Birthright program of bringing Diaspora Jewish youth to Israel, now largely subservient to Israeli right-wing themes, could have an effect, though in which direction is hard to predict. Then, too, support for Israel in the United States by evangelicals and non-Jewish Republicans, who to some extent welcome ultranationalist trends in Israel, could balance out some of the lost ground.

In sum, loss of support for Israel due to American Jewish disaffection and an increase in global anti-Semitism is likely to accelerate. But this will probably not happen so precipitously or dramatically in the course of the next decade or two as to constitute a primary factor in Israel's calculations concerning the fate of the West Bank. Nevertheless, it could be a factor, particularly if Israel's need for American Jewish support is restricted to a partial agreement with the Palestinians, a unilateral West Bank withdrawal, or merely a major disagreement with the administration in Washington.

In July 2000, as Prime Minister Ehud Barak was heading for a US-Israeli-Palestinian final-status summit at Camp David, he dispatched me to engage the American Jewish community and the media and prepare them for the possibility that he would need their support for a successful but controversial outcome at the summit negotiations. In the preceding weeks, Barak's coalition had progressively collapsed as right-wing and centrist component parties defected in protest over the prime minister's intention to reach a compromise deal with the Palestinians (note that Barak's extensive settlement construction did not help him here politically). Freshly resigned minister Natan Sharansky, a global Jewish hero for having defied Soviet anti-Semitic oppression at the cost of years in a Russian prison, was making the rounds of the American Jewish community and accusing Barak of selling out. The Israel foreign ministry, under the right-wing David Levy, was doing virtually nothing to prepare the American public for the huge financial outlays that President Bill Clinton would ask Congress to approve in order to fund the refugee-rehabilitation and water-desalination projects that Barak believed would be part and parcel of an agreement. Major American Jewish organizations were publishing full-page ads in the *New York Times* warning Barak not to "capitulate" on bread-and-butter issues like Jerusalem. Barak and his advisers were ignoring the entire scene, seemingly due to a combination of ignorance, disdain, and ineptitude.

My task, initiated at the last minute, when Barak was finally persuaded that he was risking a peace agreement through his neglect of the American Jewish public, was to talk to Jewish leaders in New York, Washington, Chicago, Los Angeles, and San Francisco and rally them to Barak's peace plan. I was stunned by what I encountered: when confronted by an official Israeli spokesman with a cogent presentation, leaders who mere days earlier had spoken out against Barak were prepared to be persuaded to voice their support openly. The media, finally sensing a coherent Israeli effort, quickly lined up with the Jewish community: one major American newspaper asked me to dictate over the phone the editorial we wanted to appear the next day.

Was it that easy to reverse American Jewish opinion? The transformation was brought home to me in Los Angeles. After I had made my pitch to an uneasy audience, one right-wing Orthodox Jewish leader stood up and addressed the others: "We knew this day would come," he said. "We fought it as long as we could. But now we have no choice but to support the elected leader of the Jewish people." I was witnessing both the strength and the weakness of the American Jewish community.

Lest we forget, Barak failed at Camp David, rendering my entire mission moot. Incidentally, he also turned down my request for a photo-op meeting prior to my departure for the United States, which would have signaled to American Jewish leaders that I truly spoke for him. In other words, my mission could, if necessary, be "denied" by a weak and vacillating lame-duck prime minister.

Now, fifteen years later, I'm not sure either my mission or the dramatic scene in Los Angeles could be repeated. The likelihood of an agreed final-status solution requiring massive American support is even lower than it proved to be back then. And the likelihood of a right-wing American Jewish leader making that speech is definitely much lower.

FIVE

The Region

Dealing with a Bad Neighborhood

Israel is surrounded by Arab Muslim states (Egypt, Saudi Arabia, Jordan, Syria) that are for the most part dictatorial, economically challenged, disdainful of human and civil rights, and corrupt. In 2015, subnational Islamist fiefdoms could be found across Israel's northern borders with Syria (al-Qaeda-linked Jabhat al-Nusra, Islamic State) and Lebanon (Hizballah) and across parts of its southern border with Egyptian Sinai (Islamic State affiliate Ansar Bayt al-Maqdis). North of the Hizballah-controlled Lebanese territory that borders on Israel is the semifunctional state of Lebanon, which can claim to be semidemocratic and multiethnic. Iranian Revolutionary Guards are deployed in southern Lebanon and southern Syria, close to Israel's borders. Iran, a Shia Muslim state, is as openly and aggressively anti-Israel, as are the Sunni Islamists of al-Qaeda and the Islamic State. And by late 2015, with Russian collaboration in Syria and the "insurance policy" of a nuclear deal with the international community, Iran was far more likely to become involved in hostilities with Israel.

Israel also borders on the West Bank–based Palestinian Authority (PA), whose last parliamentary elections, held in 2006, produced a Hamas Islamist majority that a year later took over Gaza. The PA suffers from corruption and dictatorial rule, and its human rights record is spotty: in May 2015, the Palestinian Independent Commission for Human Rights claimed that the situation was the "worst" in years. Later in 2015, the World Bank and the International Monetary Fund noted that, overall, Palestinians were getting poorer year by year. Elections are repeatedly postponed for fear of another Hamas victory, or perhaps that someone else from the anti-Hamas camp will be chosen to replace Mahmoud Abbas (Abu Mazen), who is at once president of the PA and chairman of the

Palestine Liberation Organization (PLO): in 2015 PA justice and security institutions energetically pursued Abbas's two main internal rivals, Mohammed Dahlan and Salam Fayyad, based on what appeared to be trumped-up charges of corruption. It is probably fair to say that only close security cooperation between Israeli and PA forces prevents the West Bank from descending into chaos.

Then there is, on Israel's southwestern flank, the Hamas-controlled Gaza Strip, an Islamist emirate in all but name: dictatorial, theocratic, destitute, and prone to attacking Israel periodically.

Israel has often played a negative role in the evolution of the particular circumstances at play in the two Palestinian territories. I will discuss this in chapter 6. Here we seek to place the West Bank and Gaza Strip in the broader Arab context in order to make the point that Israel is hardly to blame for all aspects of the Palestinian culture of victimhood, martyrdom, and violence. And dysfunction: by mid-2015 it was no longer possible to count the number of farcical "unity governments" set up by West Bank–based Fatah and Gaza-based Hamas, only to dissolve into oblivion ever since the Palestinian Authority's elections and the brutal Hamas takeover of the Gaza Strip split the Palestinian polity in two.

But dysfunction, martyrdom, and violence are also characteristics of the broader Arab world that surrounds Israel. That world frightens Israelis, and this has an overall negative effect on the way they perceive the prospects of coexistence with their neighbors, be they Palestinians or other Arabs. Put differently, with so many failed, fragmented, and dysfunctional states surrounding them, some Israelis may be forgiven for asking why the world assumes that, at this time, it makes sense to create yet another failed, fragmented (West Bank–Gaza), and dysfunctional state.

This explains at least in part a number of relevant trends: the decline in Israeli-Palestinian contact over recent years; the extreme sense of alienation toward Arabs taking root in the minds of most Israeli Jews since the trauma of second intifada (2000–2004) Palestinian suicide bombings targeting Israeli civilians; and, in a mirror image, the growing antagonism among West Bank Palestinians toward anything that looks like what they term "normalization" with Israelis, including not just a peace process but also dialogue projects designed to bring key sectors of both societies together to exchange ideas and become better acquainted.

With the passage of time, Israelis and Palestinians appear to seek to know less rather than more about each other. A few years ago, the Israeli and Palestinian ministries of education alike rejected an admirable attempt to juxtapose in a single high school textbook the narratives of both sides regarding the creation of Israel and the events of 1948—juxtapose, not resolve. One reason my *bitterlemons* Internet dialogue project (produced together with a Palestinian colleague) had to close in 2012 was the growing reluctance of Palestinians to participate even in "virtual" dialogue.

Among Israel's immediate neighbors, Jordan is something of an exception to this description of a negative regional environment: it has avoided major unrest and revolution, maintains a modicum of trade and tourism with Israel, and cooperates closely in managing shared security interests vis-à-vis both Palestinian terrorism and neighboring states' collapse. This explains why it is so ludicrous to hear Israeli right-wing opponents of a Palestinian state in the West Bank advocating the creation of such a state in Jordan instead. From a strategic standpoint, "Palestinizing" the Hashemite Kingdom would bring the entire hostile Arab and Iranian Middle East to the Jordan River, a fifteen-minute drive away from Jerusalem.

This was a bad neighborhood boasting semifunctional states even before the Arab revolutionary wave broke out in 2011. It was undemocratic back in March 2006 when renowned Syrian poet Adonis (Ali Ahmad Said) told Dubai TV, "If the Arabs are so inept that they cannot be democratic by themselves, they can never be democratic through the intervention of others." Since the revolutions began, many of the states have become utterly dysfunctional, with power gravitating to the hands of—and sometimes, as in Syria and Yemen, being divided between—Islamist fanatics and heavy-handed dictators.

Broadly speaking, Israel's Muslim neighbors, both Sunni and (in southern Lebanon) Shiite, including the Palestinians, reject the notion that the Jews are an indigenous Middle Eastern people who have returned to their original homeland—the founding principle of Zionism. They assert that Jews never held sovereignty in the Land of Israel (i.e., Palestine), which is *Waqf* land (an Islamic religious endowment or patrimony), hence sovereign only to Muslims. Zionism, they claim, was imposed on Palestine by the West, hence is a colonialist and imperialist movement. This is basic Islamic teaching in the Arab world's mosques.

Of course there are Muslims who, due to pragmatic leanings and/or war fatigue, are prepared to acquiesce to Israel's existence: witness the peace treaties with Egypt and Jordan. And there are Arab Muslims who, because of distance from the conflict (the Gulf emirates, Morocco) or native lifestyle (nomadic traditions that place little value on the sacred nature of land), are indifferent enough to Israel's existence to deal directly with it when convenient. Israel must treasure and cultivate these phenomena insofar as they are the only foundation available for coexistence.

But this basic teaching—the rejection of Zionism in the sense of the right of Jews to sovereignty in their historic homeland—definitely characterizes the viewpoint of the extreme Islamists, including Shiite Iran and its proxies, gathering in recent years on Israel's borders. They are not interested in dialoguing with Israel; their religious ideology dictates its destruction.

Back in the 1980s, following Egyptian-Israeli peace, a wily and experienced Egyptian diplomat named Tahsin Bashir made several visits to Israel. One of his primary messages to Israelis was that, outside of Egypt and Egyptians, the rest of the Arab Middle East consisted essentially of "tribes with flags." In recent years, with Arab revolution and anarchy surrounding us in Gaza, Syria, Libya, Iraq, and Yemen, Bashir's meaning has become very clear. The only question remaining is whether we Israelis can escape being considered yet another tribe with a flag.

Can Israel survive in such a region and remain unscathed by corruption, antidemocratic practices, ethnic discord, and extremism? Is it any wonder that most Israelis long ago discarded proposals to deal with the Palestinian issue through federative or confederative structures with Palestine and possibly Jordan? Is international criticism of the West Bank occupation and Israeli human rights standards unfair in view of regional influences?

If, for example, we make the case that the Jewish people, now restored after nearly two thousand years to its native homeland and environment, is behaving in a perfectly understandable Middle Eastern or Levantine way and should not be judged by Western standards, does this make a difference? Perhaps it does to those ultranationalist, messianist, and settler circles that place "Jewish" above "democratic" on their scale of values and seek to run the country's affairs based on their interpretation of *halacha*, or rabbinic canon law. They are still a minority in Israel, even among the 80 percent of Israelis who are Jewish. But in recent years they have, through their dynamism, devotion, and dedication, begun to play a disproportionate role in the country's affairs.

If they have their way, Israel will increasingly become part and parcel of this bad neighborhood. One astute Arab commentator, Lebanese journalist Rami Khouri, even argued in May 2015 that Arab chaos is Israel's fault: "In some ways, Israel's embrace of right-wing Zionist ethno-nationalism has been one of the propellers of the regional trend," which "seems to legitimize for others the concept of such single-identity states. Examples are South Sudan, northern Iraq, previously South Yemen, and perhaps, more radically but improbably in my view, future statelets for Sunnis, Shiites, Alawites, Christians, Druze and distinct demographic groups." Another Lebanese journalist, Michael Young, opined at the same time that "Israel is drifting towards an aggressive ethno-nationalism that often seems little different from the bigoted sectarianism raging in the Arab world."

Both Khouri and Young are Christian, and this point is probably not coincidental. Christian Arabs are more aware than most Arabs of the dangers posed by Arab extremism and more prepared than Arab Muslims to contemplate Israel as part of the region, even in a negative sense.

Meanwhile, most Jewish Israelis want their country to be Jewish and to be understood as Jewish, with a strong affinity to the Diaspora, which is almost entirely in the West, and a strong link to Western Judeo-Christian culture, with its firm foundation in the principles of justice and morality, which form part of the Hebrew contribution to civilization. In other words, they do not wish to be judged by regional standards. Most of them would define Israel as part of the West from every standpoint save geography. Indeed, with European Union member Cyprus just a half hour flight away, even geographically the West appears to be closing the distance with Israel.

This Israeli preference is particularly interesting when we note how considerable non-Western input into Israeli culture and identity has been over the decades. The prestate, pre-1948 era witnessed a strong socialist movement, characterized by the kibbutz, that drew on Eastern European communist ideology. Culturally, the Canaanite movement in the early years of Israeli statehood cultivated a pre-Hebrew, pre-Arab regional identity, while Far Left Zionists like Martin Buber and at times the Mapam party argued for a binational Jewish-Arab state. Israel survived its War of Independence in 1948 and 1949 thanks in no small part to Soviet-sponsored Czech military aid. From the mid-1950s, Israel developed strategic relationships with select non-Arab or non-Muslim Middle East states like Iran and Ethiopia—ties whose cultivation consciously drew upon the biblical-era Hebrews' ties with Persians and Ethiopians. For a short while in the mid-1950s, Israeli foreign minister Moshe Sharett tried to argue Israel's way into the nonaligned movement alongside China, India, and Indonesia, until Arab opposition thwarted the venture.

While Israel received considerable military aid from Britain and France prior to 1967, its Western orientation seemingly became more evident following the June 1967 Six-Day War, when it developed a strong strategic partnership with the United States that included aspects of Cold War cooperation and coordination against Soviet influence in the Arab Middle East. Still, peaceful relations with Egypt beginning in 1977 and, more forcefully, the advent of negotiations with the PLO, peace with Jordan, and the Madrid-based multilateral process after the fall of the Soviet Union and the First Gulf War (1990–1991) sparked a concerted effort by Israel—an effort that has largely failed—to integrate economically and even politically into the Arab region.

Most recently, the threat of Western economic sanctions against Israel because of its policies regarding the Palestinian issue has generated an effort by the Netanyahu governments to expand economic and strategic relations with India, China, and Russia—in the latter case against the backdrop of mass immigration to Israel in recent decades by Russian Jews who brought with them a strong Russian cultural and political orientation. All three of these global powers have felt free to develop strategic relations with Israel, including cooperation against militant Islam, without any overt concern beyond lip service about the state of Israeli-Palestinian relations. Netanyahu has bragged openly that India, unlike

Europe, does not place unacceptable political conditions on its relationship with Israel.

Yet Israel remains Western in orientation. Even an Israel interested in genuine economic integration into the region has to contend with the overwhelming Arab tendency to see it as a Western colonial enterprise and the Jews as an essentially Western people who maliciously usurped Muslim Arab land. Besides, there is little by way of close economic cooperation even among Arab countries: there is no Arab common market, only high customs barriers.

Then, too, Europe remains by far Israel's biggest commercial partner and the United States its dominant strategic partner. Limited strategic cooperation with Egypt, Jordan, and reportedly Saudi Arabia and the Gulf emirates against a shared Islamist threat does not translate into anything approaching a strategic relationship or a regional orientation.

True, calls by many Israeli security experts for a regional peace conference based vaguely on the Arab Peace Initiative (API) do indeed presuppose the possibility of establishing such a relationship. In some instances, these appeals are apparently based on preliminary contacts with Saudi and emirate spokespersons. But the details are agonizingly vague. The API (see chapter 8) makes demands that no rational Israeli leader can accept. By all accounts, such a relationship is impossible until Israel solves the Palestinian issue. Yet the Palestinian issue is not likely to be resolved any time soon in a manner that satisfies both a Palestinian consensus and the Arab world (or that part of it that is still functioning).

And if and when it is resolved, there is no guarantee whatsoever, and plenty of doubt, that Arab states incapable of cooperating strategically or even economically with one another will truly welcome Israel into their midst as a full partner. Indeed, as long as Islamic beliefs dictate that Arabs see Israel as an intruder on sacred Muslim territory and the Jews as a nonnation and essentially a Western religious implant, any conceivable embrace, however welcome, will remain highly tenuous.

None of this Arab attitude, coupled with the chaos that has visited most Arab countries in recent years and the overall developmental gap exhibited by most Arab states, is lost on Israelis. Then, too, in 2015, petitions by Israeli security experts supporting a "regional solution" based on the API, even when those experts number in the hundreds, tend to make a far greater impression on the rest of the world than on cynical Israelis. This also helps explain the latter's skepticism about peace.

Finally, above and beyond all else, in judging Israel's behavior the West holds Israel to its own much-trumpeted image as "the only democracy in the Middle East" possessing the "most ethical army in the world." Israeli spokespersons have a problem when they argue, at one and the same time, that Israel behaves in its wars in accordance with standards far superior to those of its enemies and that the West and its human rights organizations exercise double standards in judging Israel's behavior.

Of course what armies do when they fight, which is what they are intended to do, is by definition not "moral." Because Israel's wars are fought against enemies who seek to destroy it and as such are different than, say, Russia's wars and America's wars, there is no way to implement a comparative standard of morality. The Israel Defense Forces (IDF) should by all means continue to strive to behave humanely and ethically, but claiming the high ground of global morality is not a successful *hasbara* line (more on *hasbara*, or Israeli public diplomacy, in chapter 6).

CASE STUDY: THE SUMMER 2014 GAZA WAR

A recent case in point of negative interaction between Israeli society and a neighboring militant Islamist entity was the July–August 2014 Gaza war, known in Israel as Operation Protective Edge. Taken together, the way the war began, how the Israeli leadership managed the conflict, how the Israeli public dealt with it, and the reactions of both the "neighborhood" and the West all illustrate a number of the issues just discussed. These include the corrosive effect of the region's conflicts and violence on Israeli society and strategic thinking, growing Western intolerance of Israel's response to its enemies, and the extent of solidarity that Israel is still capable of displaying against a perceived existential enemy in an era of domestic dissonance.

Operation Protective Edge found Israelis still generally supporting a two-state solution with the Palestinians but skeptical of its feasibility and therefore not surprised at the failure, just months earlier, of a US-sponsored peace process (see chapter 7). Israelis were understandably dismayed by the anarchy and Islamist extremism sweeping the region from Libya to Iraq, including in Gaza. The public had just mourned the brutal murders of three teenage yeshiva students abducted near a West Bank settlement. In the course of the search for the three students, hundreds of Hamas supporters had been rounded up in the West Bank, while elements within the dominant religious and secular right wing of Israeli politics noticeably stepped up their advocacy, until then essentially marginal, of xenophobia and intolerance toward Arab citizens of Israel, not to mention Palestinians in the West Bank and Gaza.

Ultimately, the violent revenge murder of an East Jerusalem Arab boy by Jewish terrorists should not have surprised anyone. Nor was it surprising, subsequently, to witness the Israeli justice system seeking every possible excuse and rationale—in contrast to its prosecution of Arab terrorist murders—to exercise leniency in punishing the Jewish extremist perpetrators of that atrocity.

These events led to the outbreak in early July of yet another war with Hamas in Gaza, the third in less than six years. The public support the war generated is particularly significant when viewed against the backdrop of earlier wars. After all, Israel had moved from fighting what were perceived to be existential wars of survival against coalitions of Arab state enemies in its early decades (1948, 1967, 1973) to more controversial "wars of choice" against hostile nonstate actors implanted in ungovernable neighboring territory (1982, 2006, 2008–2009, 2012), most of which generated highly ambiguous outcomes that seemed to reflect the absence of viable strategic solutions to challenges posed by neighboring Islamist movements engaged in asymmetric warfare.

Why, then, the sweeping support for this war effort? One major factor was the percentage of Israeli civilians directly threatened by the enemy. Here we encounter a worrisome escalation that Israel is seemingly powerless to prevent. The Second Lebanon War of summer 2006 against Hizballah featured rocket attacks that targeted Israeli civilians in the northern third of the country. Leaving aside some forty ineffective missile strikes by Iraq's Saddam Hussein in 1991, this was the first time the Israeli civilian rear had been significantly attacked in war since 1948. The 2008–2009 effort against Hamas in Gaza was launched largely because extended-range rocket fire from the strip had begun to reach beyond the lightly populated Gaza periphery to the nearby Israeli coastal city of Ashkelon, with its population of one hundred thousand—a critical mass the government in Jerusalem could not ignore or dismiss.

It is notable that prior to 2008 Hamas rocket fire reached only smaller communities on the Gaza periphery, and the Israeli government chose to retaliate at a low level and not define the attacks as a major casus belli, an attitude reflecting a broadly commendable effort to avoid major warfare wherever possible. By the time we reach the Gaza conflict of 2012, we encounter for the first time very limited rocket fire on Tel Aviv and Beersheva.

In the Gaza war of July and August 2014, Hamas's rockets targeted fully two-thirds of the country, including the main population centers of greater Tel Aviv, Jerusalem, Beersheva, and Rishon LeZion. In other words, in this conflict most Israeli civilians experienced the threat of enemy attack directly for the first time, thereby generating a major incentive to support the use of any military means necessary to counter the rockets.

True, the Iron Dome antirocket missile system provided an effective defense against incoming rockets, but this was not enough to prevent disruption of normal life and in some cases major trauma. Besides, millions of Israelis, for the first time, internalized the Islamist threat: Hamas—with its virulently anti-Semitic charter that adopts the notorious czarist forgery *The Protocols of the Elders of Zion*, calls for Israel's destruction, blames the Zionists for the French and Russian revolutions and

World Wars I and II, and insists on jihad rather than peace—was trying, however ineffectually, to kill them. In parallel, the public was reassured by the fact that, unlike in 2006, the government of Israel had gone to war after considerable delay, having issued multiple warnings to Hamas to cease its rocket fire and having invoked measures to avoid Palestinian civilian casualties under extreme combat conditions and despite Hamas's persistent reliance on civilians as human shields. The public noted that Netanyahu and Defense Minister Moshe Yaalon were acting cautiously and responsibly and rebuffing demands by more extreme ministers to launch a full-fledged invasion of the strip that could prove highly costly in human lives and political repercussions. This helped rally the public, at least at the outset, behind their decision making.

Furthermore, within a week of the commencement of fighting, the public confronted a new Hamas threat: more than thirty attack tunnels dug under the Gaza border fence, with the apparent objective of launching mass terrorist raids on Israeli civilians living in border kibbutzim. Video clips of Hamas commandos emerging from below ground into Israeli territory catalyzed primordial fears. The flight of many of the kibbutz residents, who were also harried incessantly by mortar fire for which there was no early warning, presented yet another new and frightening specter with menacing overtones for the Zionist ethos of settling the land: the evacuation of civilians from pioneering border communities (not "settlements") inside sovereign Israel.

At the regional level, Israelis began to internalize the recognition that, in a largely dysfunctional Middle East state system, the country was becoming surrounded by Sunni and Shiite Islamist enemies bent not on peace and coexistence but on the country's destruction, thereby rendering this form of asymmetric warfare a kind of prototype for a new, long-term struggle against uncompromising enemies. Anti-Semitic demonstrations and attacks in Europe linked to the war reinforced the perception, certainly appropriate when applied to Hamas, that the issue was extremist hatred of Jews per se. At the same time, prominent Egyptian and even Saudi spokespersons were openly encouraging and supportive of the Israeli war effort, presenting the possibility, however tentative, that Israeli success against Hamas would, for the first time in Israel's history, cement an ad hoc regional coalition that included Israel.

The Obama administration and the US Congress were broadly supportive of Israel's motives, and European Union foreign ministers endorsed Netanyahu's war aim of demilitarizing the Gaza Strip. (This was one of several objectives enunciated helter-skelter in a manner that actually reflected a lack of cogent strategic thinking.) Israel (and the West Bank–based PLO) willingly submitted to Cairo's demand to monopolize cease-fire efforts in recognition of Egypt's support and its geopolitical centrality to future Israeli-Gazan relations. This neutralized and excluded efforts by Qatar and Turkey, both perceived in Cairo, Jerusalem, and Ramallah as supporters of Hamas, to sponsor a cease-fire.

Taken together, these developments generated the atmosphere of an existential war with important regional ramifications. Some 95 percent of Israeli Jews eventually provided sweeping support for a limited ground offensive inside Gaza aimed at finding and eradicating the tunnels, no matter what the price in IDF and other Israeli casualties and Gazan civilian losses.

Even as the war effort ground on without outcome and became increasingly ugly in terms of Palestinian civilian losses and international unease or outright condemnation, domestic Israeli and Israeli-Palestinian politics reinforced the public's readiness to support it. Netanyahu found himself balancing two opposing forces. One was extremist and pro-settler coalition elements, including some within his own party, who along with several independent strategic thinkers advocated reconquering the entire strip and physically eliminating Hamas. The other was the Zionist center (also in his coalition) and Left, including the opposition Labor Party and initially even the left-wing Meretz. The Center and Left recognized in Hamas an antipeace actor and thought they saw an opportunity to achieve by force the political reunification of Gaza with the West Bank under a PLO-led unity government that would be far better situated to command international support for renewed two-state-solution negotiations.

Here, for example, is former Meretz leader Haim Oron, a veteran peace campaigner whose son and grandson were both in combat, explaining to *Haaretz* why most on the Zionist Left grit their teeth and support the war despite the heavy damage and casualties inflicted on Gaza: "Even just wars do not purify all the terrible things that happen in them. . . . And anyone who does not experience this and understand it all the way is somewhere else and has arranged for himself a different value system than mine."

Why, then, did such a roundly supported and cautiously prosecuted war effort lead by late August to a seemingly endless round of cease-fires, cease-fire violations, and hapless four-sided negotiations (Egypt, Israel, Hamas/Islamic Jihad, and PLO/Fatah) in Cairo? Why did the outcome leave Israel with nothing approaching a decisive victory against Hamas but rather another tenuous Gaza cease-fire, yet another international investigation of alleged war crimes, and, despite Israel's rather unique readiness to supply its enemy with fuel, food, and medical supplies in wartime, growing Western and United Nations outrage over a humanitarian emergency in Gaza? Why did highly touted but sporadic statements of support for Israel by Egyptian and Saudi public figures not translate into anything overtly more substantial?

The war presented Israelis with new dilemmas and growing challenges. The country was now reluctantly prepared to accept a Palestinian

Fatah-Hamas unity government that Hamas itself quickly proved incapable of tolerating insofar as it could never bring itself to restore its
archrival Fatah (which heads the Palestinian Authority in the West Bank)
as the sovereign power in Gaza. Israel was increasingly troubled by instances of domestic intolerance and incitement between Israeli Jews and
Israeli Arabs that were incubated by the war. After two months of fighting and despite the cease-fire, it still saw no clear way forward in deter-
ring the growing Islamist threat on its borders that Hamas represents.

The sense shared by many Israelis that they had no alternative but to
fight back aggressively against Hamas may be understandable. By late
August, with the conflict dragging on, the public was increasingly suspicious of Netanyahu's much praised caution and prepared to consider a
major military offensive deep into the strip. Understandable, too, was
Israeli anger over perceived international double standards in judging
the war effort. But these emotions do not begin to explain the paradox of
this war's outcome, which generated among Israelis both doubts about
their government's perception of the events in question and resentment
toward just about the entire international community.

The most compelling explanation begins by noting that a succession of
Israeli governments has had no coherent strategy for dealing with Hamas
in Gaza. Should Israel offer to talk to Hamas? At least until 2015 Hamas
had not agreed to talk to Israel, and Egypt and the PLO—both of which
opposed cease-fire initiatives by countries friendly to Hamas—might re-
sent such an initiative on Israel's part insofar as it could be interpreted as
undercutting both Cairo's rigorous antipathy toward militant Islam and
general recognition of the PLO's exclusive leadership status among Palestinians.

Reoccupy the Gaza Strip? Toward what end? More occupation and
direct responsibility for nearly 2 million Palestinians? Quiet coexistence
with Hamas? For that to work, Israel must find a way to coexist with a
Palestinian state anchored in the West Bank, an option ostensibly
endorsed by Netanyahu but sabotaged by his ideology and settlement
policies. Besides, Hamas does not sincerely seek long-term productive
coexistence with Israel, to whose ultimate destruction it is dedicated.

Without a compelling strategy, tactics went only so far in summer
2014, especially when hard intelligence regarding the intentions of Hamas's leaders seemed to be shockingly lacking—a phenomenon unfortunately characteristic not only of Israel's understanding of most tightly
knit militant Islamist groups but also of Western and even Arab state
intelligence. Accordingly, Israel's professed goals in this war changed
constantly and erratically, from "quiet in return for quiet" to eliminating
the tunnels, to demilitarizing the Gaza Strip, to hitting Hamas hard but
leaving it in power lest more extreme Islamists replace it, and, finally, to
accepting Mahmoud Abbas's Palestinian unity government (which

would quickly prove abortive) as a potential instrument for policing and monitoring Gaza's borders.

Further, without a compelling strategy and, more pertinently, without an obviously compelling victory over Hamas, it became difficult for the government and the public to justify Israel's own painful military losses. For that matter, it was difficult for Israel to explain the far more extensive civilian losses inflicted on the Gazan population even if, ultimately, the IDF's legal team supplied persuasive explanations for those losses in terms of Hamas's own blatant violations of the rules of war.

And without a compelling strategy, Netanyahu was increasingly hard put to justify his actions to a skeptical Obama administration—one that the Israeli prime minister in any case ignored at his peril in favor of more friendly Republicans in Congress.

True, the Obama team itself made serious mistakes in this war. An early attempt by US Secretary of State John Kerry to arrange a cease-fire by bypassing Egypt and talking to Hamas supporters Turkey and Qatar was dismissed by Israelis, as well as by Egyptians, Saudis and the West Bank Palestinian leadership, as yet another instance of the US misunderstanding emerging regional dynamics. Denigrating comments about Obama, Kerry, and their handling of the war by representatives of Israel's ruling right-wing circles reflected a dangerous hubris that ignored the country's ongoing heavy dependency on Washington for everything from military supplies to a United Nations Security Council veto.

It is not easy to formulate a workable strategy for dealing with the nonstate Islamist enemies on Israel's borders. After all, they do not play by the "rules" of war or international relations. That is why sometimes even a bumbling war effort proves far more productive than it initially seems. The 2006 war effort against Hizballah was much criticized at the time inside Israel as a strategic failure; yet with the passage of years it was recognized as having deterred Hizballah from further attacks and even forced the organization's leader, Hassan Nasrallah, to live in hiding. If that is anything to judge by, the damage inflicted in 2014 on the Gaza Strip could yet generate years of deterrence and quiet, and the Israeli public could still conceivably embrace the outcome of Netanyahu's bumbling effort.

That would mean that Israel's only semi-workable strategy against Islamist nonstate actors Hizballah and Hamas, both bent on its destruction, is what defense circles euphemistically term "mowing the grass": periodically, in response to major aggression by nonstate actors based in Lebanon and Gaza, inflicting huge infrastructure damage, by the by killing many civilians, in order to reinforce, however temporarily, Israeli deterrence—yet with no hope of a political resolution. That is precisely the way the commander of Israel's Southern Command, Major General Sami Tourgeman, framed the problem less than a year after the war in a briefing to mayors of towns bordering the strip: "We must understand that once every few years there will be a round. As I understand it, the [only available option] is to create . . . periods of quiet to the extent possible."

Certainly the summer 2014 war against Gaza did not move Israel any closer to resolving its greatest strategic threat: the growing ideological/demographic danger to the country as a Jewish and democratic state. It placed additional distance between Israel and its Western support base and generated yet another round of United Nations investigations and condemnations, yet failed to compensate Jerusalem through genuinely closer strategic relations with Arab "cheerleaders" in Egypt, Saudi Arabia, Jordan, and even the Palestinian Authority, all of whom are happy to see Hamas battered but feel no consequent obligation to Israel beyond covert intelligence cooperation. Israel's handling of the summer 2014 war effort and the earlier Kerry peace initiative (see chapter 7) demonstrated that Israel's leadership has no viable plan, regionally oriented or otherwise, for stopping the disastrous multifront hemorrhaging effect of the Palestinian conflict.

Yet none of this impacted Netanyahu's electoral victory in March 2015. A large enough sector of the Israeli public refused to blame him for the summer 2014 Gaza war and its inconclusive outcome. Enough Israelis viewed the political Left and Center's more moderate approach to the Palestinian issue in general as potentially dangerous appeasement of an implacable enemy. The ongoing hostility of Israel's environs—Iran and proxies like Hizballah, along with militant Sunni Islam on the Syrian border and in Sinai and Gaza—proved a determining factor in Netanyahu's campaign.

In late June 2015 an Independent Commission of Inquiry on the Gaza Conflict, created by the United Nations Human Rights Council (UNHRC), delivered a report citing severe violations of human rights by both Israel and Hamas in the summer 2014 war. Let us ignore, for the moment, that the UNHRC's extreme anti-Israel bias is reflected in the fact that in its nine years of existence it has condemned Israel more times than the rest of the world combined. And let us ignore the fact that the commission's original chair, William Schabas, is an outspoken critic of Netanyahu and was ultimately forced to resign for having hidden a previous contractual relationship with the PLO. The two remaining commission members, both seemingly objective judges, are experts on human rights, not on war fighting and certainly not on either the military intricacies or the horrors of fighting a terrorist organization intent on killing Israeli civilians and unresponsive to the deaths of its own civilians. Then, too, the rules of war they judged this conflict by apply to wars between sovereign states, not those involving nonstate actors that never signed the Geneva Conventions.

Essentially, the commission condemned the basic Israeli military tactic for dealing with Hizballah in southern Lebanon in 2006 and Hamas in Gaza in 2014: inflict sufficiently heavy human and infrastructure losses so as to deter the militant Islamists from attacking for a relatively long time. It never even asked whether Israel has an overall political-military strategy for dealing with Gaza or, for that matter, with the West Bank.

SIX

Resolving the Palestinian Issue, 1936–2009

A Dynamic of Failure

Why have some eighty years of concerted attempts to solve this conflict failed, while many other seemingly equally intractable conflicts were resolved? This chapter is not a history of initiatives to settle the conflict. Such a narrative fills entire volumes with chronicles of seemingly endless attempts: the Peel Commission report of 1937, the 1948 war, the 1949 armistice agreements, post-1967 autonomy schemes, the Madrid negotiating structure, Oslo, attempts to involve outside actors like Jordan and the Arab League, intifadas, and a variety of track II (informal negotiating) proposals like the Geneva Accords. Rather, here we factor in the elements analyzed thus far and seek on that basis to tease out the dynamics that have repeatedly thwarted progress toward a settlement and that international intermediaries, as well as Israeli and Palestinian practitioners, generally continue to ignore, thereby virtually guaranteeing further failure.

At the outset, it is instructive to go back to 1937, when the British government's Peel Commission report attempted the first learned and reasoned analysis of the key issues dividing Jews and Arabs. The commission, formally known as the Palestine Royal Commission, was a royal commission of inquiry headed by Lord Peel. It was appointed in 1936 to investigate and report on the causes of unrest in British Mandatory Palestine, which had been rocked by an Arab general strike accompanied by Arab violence against the British authorities and the Jewish population that was fast escalating into a full-fledged armed insurrection.

The commission's summary of its observations eloquently sets the tone for this chapter and remains amazingly relevant to the contemporary issue of a two-state solution.

Chapter XX: The Force of Circumstances

The problem of Palestine is briefly restated.

Under the stress of the World War the British Government made promises to Arabs and Jews in order to obtain their support. On the strength of those promises both parties formed certain expectations.

The application to Palestine of the Mandate System in general and of the specific Mandate in particular implies the belief that the obligations thus undertaken towards the Arabs and the Jews respectively would prove in course of time to be mutually compatible owing to the conciliatory effect on the Palestinian Arabs of the material prosperity which Jewish immigration would bring in Palestine as a whole. That belief has not been justified, and there seems to be no hope of its being justified in the future.

But the British people cannot on that account repudiate their obligations, and, apart from obligations, the existing circumstances in Palestine would still require the most strenuous efforts on the part of the Government which is responsible for the welfare of the country. The existing circumstances are summarized as follows.

An irrepressible conflict has arisen between two national communities within the narrow bounds of one small country. There is no common ground between them. Their national aspirations are incompatible. The Arabs desire to revive the traditions of the Arab golden age. The Jews desire to show what they can achieve when restored to the land in which the Jewish nation was born. Neither of the two national ideals permits of combination in the service of a single State.

The conflict has grown steadily more bitter since 1920 and the process will continue. Conditions inside Palestine[,] especially the systems of education, are strengthening the national sentiment of the two peoples. The bigger and more prosperous they grow the greater will be their political ambitions, and the conflict is aggravated by the uncertainty of the future. Who in the end will govern Palestine? it is asked. Meanwhile, the external factors will continue to operate with increasing force. On the one hand in less than three years' time Syria and the Lebanon will attain their national sovereignty, and the claim of the Palestinian Arabs to share in the freedom of all Asiatic Arabia will thus be fortified. On the other hand the hardships and anxieties of the Jews in Europe are not likely to grow less and the appeal to the good faith and humanity of the British people will lose none of its force.

Meanwhile, the Government of Palestine, which is at present an unsuitable form for governing educated Arabs and democratic Jews, cannot develop into a system of self-government as it has elsewhere, because there is no such system which could ensure justice both to the Arabs and to the Jews. Government therefore remains unrepresentative and unable to dispel the conflicting grievances of the two dissatisfied and irresponsible communities it governs.

In these circumstances peace can only be maintained in Palestine under the Mandate by repression. This means the maintenance of security services at so high a cost that the services directed to "the well-being and development" of the population cannot be expanded and may even have to be curtailed. The moral objections to repression are self-evident. Nor need the undesirable reactions of it on opinion outside Palestine be emphasized. Moreover, repression will not solve the problem. It will exacerbate the quarrel. It will not help towards the establishment of a single self-governing Palestine. It is not easy to pursue the dark path of repression without seeing daylight at the end of it. . . .

The continuance of the present system means the gradual alienation of two peoples who are traditionally the friends of Britain.

The problem cannot be solved by giving either the Arabs or the Jews all they want. The answer to the question which of them in the end will govern Palestine must be Neither. No fair-minded statesman can think it right either that 400,000 Jews, whose entry into Palestine has been facilitated by the British Government and approved by the League of Nations, should be handed over to Arab rule, or that, if the Jews should become a majority, a million Arabs should be handed over to their rule. But while neither race can fairly rule all Palestine, each race might justly rule part of it.

The idea of Partition has doubtless been thought of before as a solution of the problem, but it has probably been discarded as being impracticable. The difficulties are certainly very great, but when they are closely examined they do not seem so insuperable as the difficulties inherent in the continuance of the Mandate or in any other alternative arrangement. Partition offers a chance of ultimate peace. No other plan does.

[Taken from *Report of the Palestine Royal Commission: Summary of Report*]

EXTERNAL INVOLVEMENT, FROM PEEL TO THE ARAB PEACE INITIATIVE

Over the years, a number of external actors have mediated between the two sides or facilitated their talks. These include Britain, the United States, Egypt, Jordan, Norway, and the United Nations. Some—including the United States—have tilted toward Israel; others, such as the Arab states, toward the Palestinians. But we have also witnessed well-meaning outside actors seeking to dictate the terms of a final-status agreement or even to obviate the need for one. In 1937 the Peel Commission, after listening to the parties, proposed a partition map, as did the United Nations in 1947. From 1967 to 1992, Jordan periodically undertook to negotiate the fate of the West Bank and Jerusalem or to represent the Palestinians in negotiations. Beginning with Menachem Begin's negotiations with Egypt, that country has been "offered" the Gaza Strip by Israel but has (wisely from its standpoint) backed off. The Arab Peace Initiative (API) of 2002 represents an attempt by the Arab League to dictate a set of peace parameters while offering Israel regional incentives to agree.

None of these initiatives worked. Some (the British-drawn and 1947 UN maps) were accepted by one side, the future Israel, but not by the Arab side. The API has been endorsed by the Palestine Liberation Organization (PLO) but not by a succession of Israeli governments. At one point or another, both Jordan and Egypt realized that reoccupying portions of Mandatory Palestine would burden them with a problem they would rather Israel bear.

The obvious lesson would appear to be the requirement for a mutually agreed "local" bilateral solution. But prior to 1977, none of the Arabs would negotiate directly and openly with Israel. Prior to 1993, no representative Palestinian institution agreed to do so, and the legitimacy as negotiator of the PLO, which did then agree, has in recent years been undermined by Hamas, which rejects any compromise political solution and refuses to negotiate with Israel.

So if external involvement has failed, so has direct bilateral contact.

UN INSTITUTIONAL BARRIERS

The international community has also, again with the best of intentions, created structures and institutions that have actually obstructed progress. Here are two examples.

The United Nations Relief Works Administration (UNRWA) was the first. It was created in 1949 to provide vital sustenance and support for approximately seven hundred thousand Palestinians who fled or were expelled during the 1948 war. In 1950 the United Nations created the High Commissioner for Refugees (UNHCR) to deal with all other refugee issues in the world. This duality of UN attention to refugee issues is explained by the ability of the Arab bloc in the United Nations, for years backed by the nonaligned and the Communist bloc, to fashion a special framework designed to support the Arab goal of keeping the Palestinian refugee issue "alive" as a crucial factor in any settlement of the Palestinian problem. As the late Fouad Ajami wrote, "It would have been the humane thing to tell the [Palestinian] refugees that huge historical verdicts are never overturned. But it was safer to offer a steady diet of evasion and escapism."

Note that, in parallel, Israel has absorbed millions of Jewish refugees and displaced persons—from the Holocaust, from Arab countries (about seven hundred thousand in the first four years after Israel's independence, constituting, together with the flight of Palestinians, a population exchange between Israel and the Arab states) and elsewhere throughout the world—without recourse to UN refugee facilities. And the UNHCR has overseen the resettlement of many millions of Indians, Pakistanis, Germans, Poles, and others displaced by war. Unlike all these instances, UNRWA's mandate rejects resettlement of refugees in the countries to which they fled and where they have resided ever since or in third countries that absorb immigration. The Arab countries insist the Palestinian refugees' fate be agreed between Israel and the PLO, yet without "patriation" or permanent settlement in their countries of residence—a principle enshrined as late as 2002 in the Arab Peace Initiative and ratified annually ever since.

Meanwhile, uniquely among global refugee issues, the count of certified Palestinian refugees expands from generation to generation, today exceeding 5 million. It is by now axiomatic among all but the more extreme Palestinians (e.g., Hamas) that Israel cannot possibly repatriate all, most, or even a large fraction of the refugees within a final-status framework; even PLO leader Mahmoud Abbas acknowledged as much in a 2008 cable leaked by Al Jazeera among the so-called Palestine Papers. Put differently, it is understood that the demand that Israel accept 5 million Palestinian refugees, all but a few thousand of whom were not even born in what is today Israel, is in effect a demand to "Palestinize" Israel that no Israeli negotiator will accept. (As for the persistent and very significant demand that Israel recognize all the refugees' right to return, see the next section.)

Still, in the face of genuine hostility and heavy livelihood restrictions in countries like Lebanon, UNRWA ministers to refugees' health, welfare, and education, never questioning the principle of descendants inheriting refugee status and never countering the right-of-return narrative with a demand for Arab host countries or other countries outside the region to absorb the refugees and grant them full citizenship. (As with other Palestinian issues, Jordan is the exception here, having awarded full citizenship status to its Palestinian refugee population.)

UNRWA does its job well. Back in 1967, when Israel conquered the Gaza Strip, with its huge refugee population ensconced in squalid camps, a number of Israeli decision makers broached the idea of expelling UNRWA from Gaza. After all, the UN body was seen as the virtual embodiment of all that was wrong with the world's unique perpetuation of this refugee issue. But official Israel backed down once it realized that without UNRWA, it would become responsible for the welfare of these refugees, at a huge cost, and that only an end-of-conflict solution to the Palestinian issue could remove the Gaza refugees from the agenda of Israeli-Palestinian relations.

So Israel and UNRWA coexist uneasily, while the refugee problem that UNRWA helps perpetuate remains the elephant in the room of Israeli-Palestinian relations and UNRWA firmly reflects Arab and Palestinian positions at the local level. In Gaza many of its employees are seconded to it by Hamas; Israeli authorities regularly expose the anti-Semitic tweeting and Facebook postings of UNRWA employees. In the summer 2014 Israel-Hamas war, it emerged that Hamas had used UNRWA facilities to store ordnance and had even fired rockets at Israel from them. On the other hand, Israel scored indiscriminate artillery and bombing hits even on UNRWA installations that were not abused by Hamas, killing scores of civilians who had taken shelter there and thereby exacerbating an already problematic relationship.

A telling reminder of the centrality of UNRWA and the refugee issue was provided in April 2015 when, in the midst of the Syrian civil war, Islamic militants conquered the Yarmouk Palestinian refugee camp near Damascus. Yarmouk was once the largest such camp administered by UNRWA, its population numbering around 350,000, equivalent to half of the original 1948 Palestinian refugee count. After bitter fighting, by 2015 there remained only some eighteen thousand miserable refugee noncombatants. While UNRWA was trying valiantly to bring them vital supplies, Arab citizens of Israel from the Galilee, some of whom had distant cousins in Yarmouk (whose original Palestinian population in 1948 was from nearby northern Israel), argued publicly that Israel was somehow responsible for Yarmouk's current plight and was obliged, nearly seventy years after their grandfathers had fled Israel's bitter War of Independence, to help them.

This was Palestinian politics of martyrdom at its height. No one suggested that the mess at Yarmouk was the responsibility of Arab countries. But why should they? Arab countries had been manipulating the Palestinian issue for decades rather than displaying compassion for Palestinians.

During a similar crisis at Yarmouk a year or two earlier, Israeli prime minister Benjamin Netanyahu had agreed that the Palestinian Authority (PA) could absorb victims of the Syrian fighting in and around Yarmouk if those refugees declared that by settling in Ramallah, Jericho, or Khan Yunis they had fulfilled "return" and would have no further claims on Israel. Hamas in Gaza refused outright to accept the refugees. West Bank–based Palestinian leader Mahmoud Abbas agreed but rebuffed the demand regarding renunciation of further "return," reportedly stating, "It's better they die in Syria than give up their right of return." Jordan didn't want to let them traverse its territory.

Thus has the Yarmouk camp in recent years effectively symbolized the intractability of the Palestinian refugee issue. Yet Yarmouk also represents the interaction of two historic Middle East refugee crises: that of 1948 and another created, particularly but not only in Syria, by the Arab revolutions that began in 2011 and have brought a number of dysfunctional countries to the verge of total collapse under the burden of millions of refugees and displaced persons. A wise and far-reaching international strategic approach would at this point recognize the desperate need for a single UN body with extensive responsibility and capacity to resettle and rehabilitate the cumulative refugee population of the entire region. The pro-Palestinian lobby at the United Nations can be counted on to thwart such an initiative.

A second and very different but problematic UN creation is Security Council Resolution 242 of November 1967. That resolution provided the "territories-for-peace" formula that guided Israel's peace agreements with Egypt (1979) and Jordan (1994), an abortive agreement with Lebanon (1983), and an almost-agreement with Syria (1995, 2000). But 242, enacted only months after Israel occupied large Palestinian populations in the West Bank, East Jerusalem, and the Gaza Strip, studiously said nothing about the Palestinians. It mentioned "refugees" but not Palestinian refugees.

Resolution 242 was good for peace between Israel and neighboring Arab states. It was bad for the Palestinian issue, which to this day suffers from the absence of a parallel set of UN-defined principles for solving it. True, the PLO eventually endorsed 242, thereby giving it a theoretical claim to represent Palestinians in a territories-for-peace deal after Jordan waived its 242 rights in the West Bank in 1988. And 242 calls for Israel to "withdraw from territories" captured during the war, a formula universally understood to mean the West Bank as well as Sinai, Gaza, and the Golan, though the conspicuous absence of "the" before territories means that perhaps a West Bank withdrawal could involve some territorial changes in Israel's favor. But this could not entirely negate the logic underlying repeated Israeli government claims that the West Bank and Gaza were not conquered from any Arab country whose sovereignty there had been recognized prior to 1967; accordingly, the territories were "disputed" and not "occupied" (at least as international law defines occupation in the Fourth Geneva Convention), they could be settled by Israelis, and 242 did not fully apply to them.

The United Nations created Israel from the standpoint of international law, thereby giving Israel more international legitimacy than many countries. The United Nations has policed many truces and cease-fires between Israel and its Arab neighbors and contributed positively to Israel's well-being in numerous ways. But it has also clearly been an obstacle, and not only by means of UNRWA and because of the absence of an Israel-Palestine version of 242. Remember the General Assembly's "Zionism Is Racism" resolution of 1975, negating the raison d'être of a member state. And note a whole series of institutions like the UN Committee on the Exercise of the Inalienable Rights of the Palestinian People and an annual parade of anti-Israel resolutions in a variety of UN bodies that have the effect of painting Israel as the world organization's primary problem and preoccupation—and send this message to the entire international community, to the detriment of serious efforts for peace.

1967 AS WATERSHED: PRE- AND POST-1967 ISSUES
AND THE NARRATIVE GAP

Israel could make peace with Egypt and Jordan based on 242, but not with the Palestinians. Their conflict with the state of Israel begins in 1948, with their humiliating flight and expulsion from their homeland. They did not fight Israel in 1967 and did not "lose" a war or territory then. Quite the contrary, the 1967 defeat and retreat of Jordan and Egypt set the scene for the Palestinians to claim, or reclaim, at least a portion of pre-1948 Mandatory Palestine.

Thus, uniquely in the annals of Arab-Israel peacemaking, the direct Palestinian-Israeli negotiations that commenced officially in 1993 focus on both pre-1967 and post-1967 issues. The former, as understood by Palestinians, concern the question of the return of some or all 1948 refugees to Israel and the "right of return" of all—two related but different issues, which we shall rejoin. They also touch on the question of ownership and control of holy places, particularly the Temple Mount or Haram al-Sharif in the heart of Jerusalem, an issue that is not merely pre-1967 but in some ways goes back hundreds and even thousands of years, to the building of the First Temple by the ancient Hebrews and the construction on its ruins of al-Aqsa Mosque by the early Muslims.

In contrast, the post-1967 issues to be resolved by Israelis and Palestinians parallel those resolved in peace talks between Israel and Egypt and Israel and Jordan: borders, security, the fate of settlements. Even the Palestinian demand for a capital in Arab East Jerusalem may be considered a post-1967 issue insofar as it concerns borders and sovereignty, even if many Israelis would insist that anything touching on Jerusalem is somehow a "narrative" (hence pre-1967) issue. Here we must note that hardliners among the Israeli right wing are in part responsible for undermining the negotiating centrality of the post-1967 issues insofar as they reject the 1967 lines in favor of the demand to annex or at least continue to control the entire West Bank and all of East Jerusalem.

By and large, the direct final-status negotiations in and around Camp David in 2000 and between Prime Minister Ehud Olmert and Palestinian leader Mahmoud Abbas in 2008 (the Annapolis process), as well as discussion of third-party formulae like the Clinton parameters of late 2000, have registered an encouraging degree of progress on post-1967 issues. When these discussions broke off, there remained narrow and seemingly negotiable gaps regarding the location of the border, the scope of land swaps to compensate Palestinians for Israeli annexation of settlement blocs, the parameters of security arrangements, and even the location of a Palestinian capital. Even the Kerry-led indirect talks of 2013 and 2014 were said to have registered some progress on territorial issues.

This has not been the case in negotiations over the pre-1967 issues. Even when the two sides agreed to bargain over numbers of 1948 refugees whose repatriation Israel might accept, albeit with numerical gaps in the tens of thousands, they never came close to agreeing on a verbal formula that Palestinians would recognize as Israeli acceptance, even if only in principle, of the right of return of all 5 million "refugees," most of whom are children and grandchildren of refugees, were not born in Israel, and have never lived there.

Here it bears noting that the Palestinian rejection of the Clinton parameters proposed by outgoing US president Bill Clinton in December 2000 focused on a refusal to compromise regarding precisely the pre-1967 issues of refugees and Jerusalem holy places.

These pre-1967 narrative issues derive from the circumstances of Israel's origins as a state and the parallel Palestinian dispersal. The huge and seemingly immovable abyss separating the positions of Israelis and Palestinians on these issues is unique to their conflict alone. Israelis understand the right of return of 1948 refugees as a demand to undermine their country as a Jewish state and to deny its legitimacy. Israelis understand the Arab world's nurturing of successive generations of refugees, now numbering over 5 million, as support for the Palestinian position. Palestinians understand the right of return as the ultimate affirmation of their narrative holding that Israel is a foreign entity "created in sin" by outside forces — that Israel does not represent a legitimate Jewish national movement at all. Even the many Palestinians who concede that actual "return" is impractical insist on getting what one may term the psychohistorical satisfaction of Israel acknowledging its "guilt." And they readily admit that this is the Israel they will present to future generations in school textbooks.

Some years ago Dr. Khalil Shikaki, a leading Palestinian opinion researcher, polled Palestinian refugees throughout the Middle East and discovered that only about 10 percent, or four hundred thousand (the ever-expanding refugee total cited by UNRWA was then around 4 million), would insist on actual return to the state of Israel under a two-state solution. When I asked Shikaki, himself the son of a refugee from southern Israel, why his survey had not inquired what percentage of Palestinian refugees insist on their right of return as opposed to actual return, he replied, "No need to ask. The principle of right of return is universally accepted among the refugees." Nor can we take for granted that, if and when return of the four hundred thousand were to commence, the remaining millions and their descendants would not change their minds based on Israel's formal acceptance of their "right."

Regarding the Temple Mount/Haram al-Sharif, many Palestinians, in a dramatic reversal of classic Muslim historiography, deny there is a Hebrew legacy there at all. Again, Israelis view this denial as a negation of Jewish national and religious roots in the Holy Land — two successive temples on the Mount in the pre-Christian era that served as the focus of Hebrew national and spiritual life for centuries. Note, too, that the PLO has repeatedly leveraged a huge anti-Israel majority in the United Nations Educational, Scientific and Cultural Organization (UNESCO) to have the entire Temple Mount, much of which consists of open courtyards and gardens that lie above the ruins of the two temples, declared as a mosque, thereby rendering any Israeli activity there whatsoever a "violation."

Israel's demand for recognition as a Jewish state (this is the terminology of UN General Assembly Resolution 181 of 1947 creating the state of Israel; it was embodied in Israel's Declaration of Independence less than a year later) is very much a response, championed in Israel by the political Right (and others), to these Palestinian positions. Not surprisingly, an examination of attempts to produce an agreed two-state solution since 2000 (Camp David, the Clinton parameters, Taba, the informal Geneva Accords, Olmert-Abbas, and so forth) indicates that discussions of the pre-1967 issues have produced virtually no narrowing of differences. Indeed, these issues are not even clearly defined in the agreed 1993 Oslo Declaration of Principles, and only in the course of final-status talks did the two sides become fully aware of each other's narratives and the differences separating them (e.g., by Yasser Arafat and Mahmoud Abbas declaring at Camp David in 2000 that "there never was a temple on the Temple Mount" and Israel demanding recognition since then as a Jewish state).

"NOTHING IS AGREED UNTIL EVERYTHING IS AGREED"

Although not written into the Oslo Accords, this mantra has become a central tenet of all negotiations associated with implementation of Oslo since 1993. The logic is plain: Israel can agree tentatively to a concession on, say, a Palestinian capital in East Jerusalem or the 1967 lines, but it cannot agree conclusively until it ascertains that its concession is balanced by a Palestinian concession on, say, the right of return or who owns the Temple Mount. But the upshot has been negative: the two sides could conceivably agree on 95 percent of the issues at stake in final-status talks; yet negotiations would collapse and all concessions by both sides would be erased from the protocol due to disagreement over the remaining 5 percent.

Of special note is the fact that "nothing is agreed until everything is agreed" has become a key element in the muddling of pre- and post-1967 issues, even though "mixing" the two in this way is the equivalent of confounding apples and oranges.

SOVEREIGN STATE VERSUS NATIONAL
LIBERATION MOVEMENT

Not only does the Palestinian issue present peacemakers with pre-1967 narrative challenges that do not and did not constitute impediments to end-of-conflict agreements with neighboring Arab states, but it also places on the two sides of the negotiating table a sovereign state, Israel, and a national liberation movement, the Palestine Liberation Organization. This makes negotiating more difficult than in a state-to-state model.

The PLO, after all, aspires to represent far more than a finite population in a clearly defined territory. It represents the Palestinian diaspora, which is more numerous than the Arab residents of the West Bank, Gaza Strip, and East Jerusalem put together and is dispersed primarily, but not solely, among several Arab states: Jordan, Lebanon, and Syria. In some instances (see chapter 7), the PLO aspires to represent the interests of Palestinian Arab citizens of Israel as well. Even if we discount the right-of-return issue that constitutes the primary focus of diaspora Palestinian aspirations, the nonstate nature but multistate geography of the PLO's constituency creates a problematic imbalance in negotiations: the PLO is negotiating not just the fate of the West Bank, East Jerusalem, and the Gaza Strip, conquered in 1967, but also the fate of millions of diaspora third- and fourth-generation "refugees" whose vision of an end-of-conflict solution involves not merely those territories but sovereign post-1948/pre-1967 Israel as well, meaning the total Palestinization of Israel.

Little wonder, then, that some Israelis have emerged from negotiations with the distinct impression that the Palestinian side prefers the status of eternal martyr and victim over the compromises necessary to achieve some sort of statehood. From the Palestinian standpoint, it's not that simple.

The advent in the mid-1990s of the Palestinian Authority, exercising limited governance over a number of defined West Bank and Gazan territories, did not change this reality because the Oslo Accords specify that the PLO, not the PA, represents the Palestinians in final-status negotiations with Israel. From this standpoint, negotiations would undoubtedly be much easier if the PA or even the entire West Bank and Gaza Strip were recognized as the "state" Israel must negotiate final status with (with land swaps, security arrangements, and so forth). Indeed, even Israeli and Palestinian officials occasionally refer erroneously to the PA as Israel's final-status negotiating partner.

Here the 2005 unilateral Israeli withdrawal from the Gaza Strip offers a special case. There are no longer Israeli settlers or soldiers in the strip, and Israel does not interfere with the strip's border with an Arab country, Egypt. Hence in the eyes of most Israelis, Israel no longer occupies Gaza, and the strip may be considered to have the characteristics of a state. But for years Egypt has kept its Gaza border closed to a far greater extent than has Israel, due to Cairo's animosity toward the Hamas Islamist movement ruling the strip. And even though Hamas has launched major rocket attacks on Israeli civilian concentrations periodically since 2007, when it took power in the strip by force, most of the world has continued to insist that Israel "occupies" Gaza and is obliged to negotiate its fate with the PLO, which has no foothold there.

Gaza offers another important object lesson for the Palestinians' statehood aspirations in negotiations. When Israel withdrew unilaterally in 2005, the PLO still governed Gaza, and the border with Egypt was open. Despite PLO refusal to negotiate the modalities of Israel's departure with the Ariel Sharon government, arrangements were made for massive international aid to help turn the strip into a model of Palestinian statebuilding. In the eyes of most Israelis, the PLO failed utterly to make good on this opportunity. Not for the first time, the Palestinians have endless excuses involving betrayal by external actors.

Apropos blaming others, the late Abba Eban, Israel's longtime UN ambassador, complained decades ago that "the Palestinians never miss an opportunity to miss an opportunity." He was referring to a phenomenon whereby the Palestinian leadership rejects each offer of territorial compromise only to realize, too late, that the next offer awards the Palestinians even less territory, beginning with the Peel Commission (which dealt with two national liberation movements, Jewish and Arab, of which the Jewish was prepared to compromise), which gave the Palestinian state and a neutral Jerusalem corridor fully 80 percent of Mandatory Palestine, through the 1947 UN offer of 55 percent, the 1978 Camp David offer of autonomy throughout the West Bank and Gaza Strip, and the 2000 and 2008 final-status offers by Israeli leaders that have in many ways been superseded by the ongoing spread of settlements.

The real issue here is Palestinian negotiating strategy, which operates as a function of the Palestinians' narrative of victimhood and injustice inflicted upon them by the entire Zionist enterprise. The international community has repeatedly recognized Zionism—when the League of Nations ratified the Balfour Declaration and the United Nations voted to create a Jewish state in Mandatory Palestine—as the legitimate expression of the Jewish people's right to self-determination in its ancestral homeland. Yet Palestinian Arab opposition to Zionism has from the very outset rejected every aspect of this statement: the Jews are not a people, but rather a bunch of coreligionists; as a nonpeople, they have no right to self-determination, but rather were implanted in Palestine by Western imperialism; Palestine is the ancestral homeland not of Jews, but rather of Arabs and Muslims.

If you are convinced of the justice of the Palestinian position, then you consistently reject compromise on the grounds that it is inherently unjust. You adjust your narrative accordingly—for example, asserting that there never was a Hebrew temple on the Temple Mount/Haram al-Sharif in the heart of Jerusalem, even though for hundreds of years, until around a century ago when Zionism made its appearance, your historiography had recognized that the mosques on the Mount were built on the ruins of the Second Temple precisely in order to reinforce the claim of Islam to supersede Judaism.

And if, in the late 1980s and early 1990s, you reluctantly conclude that Israel is so strong and so permanent that you have to compromise in order to salvage something for Palestinians, then you come to the negotiating table to discuss final-status issues, beginning at Camp David in 2000, with an announcement that you have made the ultimate compromise on your claim to undisputed sovereignty over all of Palestine by recognizing Israel's existence—as a sovereign state albeit not a Jewish state—within the 1948–1967 boundaries. Having conceded your claim to 72 percent of the territory west of the Jordan River, you can contemplate no further territorial compromises, and any West Bank or Jerusalem land Israel wants to annex must be balanced by equivalent Israeli territorial compromises that preserve the 72–28 proportionality. From the standpoint of the Palestinian narrative and consequent mind-set, relinquishing 72 percent of the land you believe is yours is indeed a huge sacrifice.

Further, if you argue that even the remaining 28 percent of the land is not yet yours but is under some form of occupation, and you recall that you (the PLO leadership) are a liberation organization and not a state, then you continue to glorify terrorists who attacked Israeli "occupiers" by naming central squares in Ramallah after them, and you refuse to condemn new terrorist acts in the West Bank or rocket firings from Gaza. You do all this, while making sure your security services continue to cooperate with Israel in rooting out West Bank and even East Jerusalem terrorists, lest they turn on your own fragile rule in Ramallah.

Contrast this strategy with Israel's. Israel has been prepared to compromise on territory from the outset, in 1922, when the British detached Transjordan from the Mandate, and again in 1937, with the Peel plan, when the *Yishuv* (the prestate Jewish community in Palestine) accepted only 20 percent of the remaining territory. Jewish state-building recognized compromise from the beginning; the Zionist narrative is built on compromise and improvisation.

I am not arguing here that Jewish and Israeli compromise is "right" and Palestinian obstinacy "wrong." Each side has persuasive grounds for believing in its narrative. My point, rather, is that the gap between their respective approaches creates an enormous cognitive obstacle to negotiations. Yet this is not the only element of dissonance the parties have encountered in their dealings.

APPALLING IGNORANCE OF THE OTHER SIDE'S
POSITIONS AND SENSITIVITIES

Considering how much time Israelis and Palestinians have clocked negotiating with one another, it is striking to note the degree of ignorance of
the other side's positions and sensitivities each has displayed when fac-
ing off in the most advanced discussions of final status. Here are several
examples that reflect both ignorance of the other side's view of the issues
and (a corollary?) poor negotiating skills.

At the July 2000 Camp David negotiations, Israeli prime minister
Ehud Barak reportedly sought to secure Palestinian agreement to a compromise arrangement on the Temple Mount whereby a synagogue would
be constructed on the far northeastern "lip" of the mount, overlooking
the site of the biblical Holy of Holies, as a symbolic expression of the
Jewish people's link to the site without in any way infringing on the
mosques. He had secured the consent of several prominent rabbis to this
arrangement, which in any case reflected centuries-old rabbinic objections to Jews actually setting foot on the site of the Temple for fear of
inadvertently treading on the forbidden Holy of Holies. But because his
governing coalition was collapsing and he feared malicious leaks of his
negotiating positions prior to the Camp David meeting, Barak had not
tested this proposition informally on senior Palestinians.

When he presented it, the Palestinians greeted the proposal with consternation: the Jews, they felt certain, were attempting to establish a foothold on the Mount in preparation for taking it over and building a new
temple in place of the mosques. Hadn't UNESCO agreed that the entire
Mount was a mosque? Besides, as both Yasser Arafat and Mahmoud
Abbas stated at Camp David (and Abbas has repeated ever since), "There
never was a temple on the Temple Mount."

And why consternation? A few weeks after the failure of Camp David
2000, I discussed this with Palestinian political scientist Khalil Shikaki,
whom Arafat had charged with collecting the individual recollections of
each of the twelve Palestinian participants (the American conveners did
not maintain a written protocol at Camp David). "What is the most prominent impression or lesson from your efforts?" I asked Shikaki. He replied, "We had absolutely no idea how important Haram al-Sharif [the
Temple Mount] is to Israelis."

Inexcusable American ignorance also characterized Camp David 2000.
The conveners understood the Palestinian position regarding the Temple
Mount no better than the Israeli side did. As the talks were convening,
they initiated a crash course with Israeli (and possibly Palestinian) experts to bring their negotiators up to par. Nor did they take steps to
prepare Arab leaders to support a possible compromise Palestinian position regarding a capital in Jerusalem and control of the holy places (see
"Linkages" below). As a consequence, at the critical juncture when the

US administration appealed to them to intervene with the Palestinian delegation, Arab leaders in capitals like Cairo felt estranged and showed no readiness to ease Arafat into even minor concessions regarding Jerusalem.

If a distressing lacuna regarding the need for quiet prenegotiations characterized Barak's approach to the Temple Mount at Camp David, Ehud Olmert displayed a parallel inexcusable arrogance at the negotiating table. Olmert himself relates that at the final session of the Olmert-Abbas final-status talks in September 2008, he presented to Abbas the principles of a comprehensive agreement, based on his understanding of Abbas's positions as laid out in many months of previous one-on-one discussions in Jerusalem.

By any previous and subsequent Israeli standards, and to Olmert's credit, his offer was the farthest-reaching by Israel on record. After outlining the proposal and showing Abbas the document laying it out in detail, Olmert demanded that Abbas sign it on the spot. When Abbas asked to take it with him, study it, and show his advisers Olmert's map of final-status borders, land swaps, and a Palestinian capital in East Jerusalem, Olmert refused: take it or leave it, he said. Abbas left it, never came back, and later complained to the *Washington Post*'s Jackson Diehl, "The gaps [between the Israeli and Palestinian positions] were wide," something he apparently never said directly to Olmert himself and never properly explained elsewhere. Incidentally, Abbas's request to study the proposal may be understood as reasonable in principle, except that practical experience with Palestinian negotiators suggests that this should have been understood as the equivalent of a Palestinian no.

Another example of Israeli arrogance and ignorance concerns the status of the settlers who might "remain behind" in the territory of a Palestinian state. The issue came up in talks between the settler leadership and Arafat's representatives that I convened in 1995 (see preface). The settlers, contemplating a worst-case scenario in which Israel agreed to the creation of a Palestinian state in nearly all of the West Bank, suggested that the settlements could retain an ex-territorial status as Israeli enclaves inside Palestine protected by Israeli police or soldiers.

Hassan Asfour, one of Arafat's designated negotiators, replied, "There is no room in our region for ethnically 'pure' states." Then he added,

> An Israeli who wishes to live within the state of Palestine will be a Palestinian citizen, not a "resident." We'll also permit dual Israeli-Palestinian citizenship. We don't want any discrimination, we want a democratic country. The presence of Jews will help us ensure democracy, and will also enable us to serve as a bridge between Israel and the Arab world. As for the settlements per se, they are a consequence of occupation. Where their location doesn't constitute a problem for us, we'll consider the possibility of leaving them in place. But not before a Palestinian state comes into being in Gaza and the West Bank. Kiryat

Arba [a settler town adjacent to Hebron], for example, was created as
part of the occupation. A settler can remain there as an individual, but
the Jewish municipality will disappear, and Kiryat Arba will merge
administratively with Arab municipal units.

Note that Asfour was speaking twenty years ago, before political Islam
challenged the PLO's ideological hegemony, and that, as an ex-Commu-
nist, he was pledged to support both the two-state idea and the notion of
ethnic pluralism—principles endorsed in their day by Soviet teachings.
Even in his thoroughly logical scheme, which provided a mirror image of
the status of Palestinian Arab citizens of Israel, settlements that remained
would be subject to Palestinian police and Palestinian courts—an almost
certain formula for escalating tensions. In contrast, in today's reality, the
Palestinian approach would almost certainly be less lenient due to Islamist influence, the far greater number of settlements and settlers, and the
bad blood of twenty more years of hostility.

In any event, the settler presumption (shared at the time by many
others in Israel, including in the peace camp) that the presence of settlements could constitute a territorial exception to Palestinian rule demonstrated ignorance regarding a fundamental Palestinian requirement for
resolving the conflict: the dignity of genuine sovereignty. The Peel report
stated it well in paraphrasing Arab testimony to the Peel Commission:
"You say my house has been enriched by the strangers who have entered
it. But it is my house, and I did not invite the strangers in, or ask them to
enrich it, and I do not care how poor or bare it is if only I am master in it."

Interestingly, Israeli ignorance of the Arab narrative was not always
the case. Here is David Ben Gurion's testimony from a June 1919 speech:
"Everybody sees a difficulty in the question of relations between Arabs
and Jews. But not everybody sees that there is no solution to this question. No solution! There is a gulf, and nothing can fill that gulf. . . . I do
not know what Arab will agree that Palestine should belong to the
Jews. . . . And we must recognize this situation. . . . We, as a nation, want
this country to be ours; the Arabs, as a nation, want this country to be
theirs."

Here is another, later example of ignorance surrounding the two
sides' basic understanding of one another. In a prime-time interview on
Israeli television in 2012, the nearly eighty-year-old Abbas volunteered
that as a native of Safed, an ancient city in northern Israel from which he
had fled as a boy in 1948, he had no intention of asking to "return" there
under an agreed two-state solution. Israel's Channel 2 news trumpeted
this as a major Palestinian concession, and many Israelis jumped to the
conclusion that Abbas had given up the right of return on behalf of all
Palestinians. Within twenty-four hours this misunderstanding obliged
the Palestinian leader's office to issue a correction: Abbas had foregone
the right of return for himself only; he could not speak for Palestinians at

large, who continued to enjoy that right. Thus did a well-meaning but minor statement by an aging Palestinian leader and the ignorance of his interviewers actually help widen the gap between Israelis and Palestinians on this supersensitive issue.

Finally, the issue of incitement reflects mutual ignorance. Over the years since the Oslo process began, each side has accused the other of incitement. At various junctures, joint commissions have been set up to monitor alleged incitement by both. None of this has made much of a difference, and incitement continues to cloud perceptions and poison the atmosphere.

The biggest problem appears to be defining incitement. Israel accuses the PLO and PA of circulating maps in which it does not exist: "Palestine" runs from the Mediterranean to the Jordan. Yet the map of the Israeli daily weather forecast also erases the green line and renders the entire territory a single entity. Each side denies its own incitement while accusing the other. Each has religious extremists who regularly preach the most horrific things about the other. Each complains about the other's extremism while dismissing its own as falling into the category of folklore.

Is settlement construction incitement? The Palestinians think so. Is naming a square in Ramallah in honor of a suicide bomber incitement? Israelis are certain it is. Are these asymmetric examples? Both would agree they are but would not concur about anything else in this paradigm.

It is true that negative Islamist images that deny Israel's right to exist and denigrate Jews are far more widespread throughout the Muslim world, including Palestine, than negative Jewish images of Palestinians and Arabs. But neither side makes a serious effort to clean up its act, and this affects the attitudes of new generations. Indeed, as the conflict becomes increasingly religious and tribal rather than political, the situation can only get worse.

LINKAGES

Not only does the Palestinian side in negotiations with Israel have to constantly factor in the interests of the Palestinian diaspora, but it also operates under a significant degree of tension with the Arab world regarding the refugee/right-of-return issue and holy places. Here there is no symmetry with Israel, which is free to decide on the basis of its assessment of its own interests. As the widely recognized leader of the Jewish world, its prime minister generally does not feel obliged to bow to the will of the Jewish Diaspora concerning, say, the fate of sites holy to Jews everywhere.

I already mentioned, in the context of Camp David 2000, the linkage between Palestinian demands regarding Jerusalem and those of the Arab and Muslim worlds. Is a Palestinian leader free to make the smallest concession regarding Jewish claims to the Temple Mount without consulting the Arab League and global Muslim groups? Almost certainly not, insofar as a Palestinian state will be beholden to Saudi Arabia, guardian of the two holiest sites of Islam, Mecca and Medina, for long-term financial aid and will want its Temple Mount caretaker status recognized by all Muslims. Then, too, the 1994 Israel-Jordan peace treaty awards the Hashemite Kingdom the primary role of guardian of the Muslim holy places in Jerusalem, thereby introducing another actor into negotiations regarding the Temple Mount.

Then there is linkage regarding the refugee/right-of-return issue. In negotiating with Israel, the PLO claims to represent the interests of millions of Palestinian refugees, some of whom (in Lebanon, for example), are stateless and bereft of most rights, whereas others, as in Jordan, are citizens of another Arab country. Moreover, the Arab League's Arab Peace Initiative, to which the PLO subscribes, proffers a formula whereby the refugee issue will be the subject of an "agreed" solution (between Israel and the PLO) and will be resolved based on UN General Assembly Resolution 194 of 1949.

Note that 194 never uses the expression "right of return"; yet all Arabs claim to understand it somehow to guarantee that right. The API itself does not mention the right of return, nor does Israel agree to that demand. Yet paragraph 4 of the API "assures the rejection of all forms of Palestinian patriation which conflict with the special circumstances of the Arab host countries." This means there can be no naturalization and permanent settlement of hundreds of thousands of refugees in their countries of residence (primarily Lebanon and Syria but possibly also Jordan, where they number in the millions and even have citizenship) and implies that they must either return to Israel or immigrate to a third country.

Given all these Arab third-party conditions and counterconditions regarding holy places and the right of return, how is even the most moderate and compromise-minded Palestinian leader supposed to navigate these issues in final-status talks aimed at resolving all claims between Palestinians and Israelis?

Another form of linkage that has never gotten off the ground is a series of Israeli proposals that Egypt, Jordan, and Syria in some way agree that their sovereign territory will be involved in a Palestinian territorial solution—for example, by expanding the Gaza Strip into Sinai for demographic reasons. None of Israel's Arab neighbors has ever evinced a readiness to involve its territory in this way to facilitate a solution, even when the Israeli parties presenting the proposal have suggested compensatory territorial swaps.

Incidentally, linkage between the Palestinians and the Arab League can work both ways. In February 2015 Martin Indyk, who administered the 2013–2014 final-status talks on behalf of US Secretary of State John Kerry, told a conference in Tel Aviv that he and Kerry had persuaded no fewer than six key Arab leaders to provide "cover," or legitimization, for Abbas if he would agree to recognize Israel as a Jewish state. When Kerry and Indyk informed Abbas of this "breakthrough," he said nothing. Instead, he proceeded to travel to Arab League headquarters in Cairo and extract a resolution, approved by all twenty-two league members, rejecting the Jewish state demand.

Finally, there is the prisoner-release issue. Over the decades, Israel has released thousands of convicted Palestinian terrorists as part and parcel of both interim peace deals with the PLO and prisoner exchange deals with Hamas, Hizballah, and other extreme movements (including the pre-Oslo Lebanon-based PLO). In 2011, Israel released over one thousand terrorists in exchange for a single Israeli soldier, Gilad Shalit, held by Hamas. The general response of a significant portion of the Israeli public to these releases and exchanges is to claim that Israel is being extorted and paying too high a price: the resultant peace deals never materialize, too many of the freed prisoners fall back into their terrorist ways, and the Palestinian public and even its most moderate leaders tend to glorify the terrorists as folk heroes. What should be a confidence builder between the sides has the opposite effect.

INFORMAL "TRACK II" TALKS

One of the singular characteristics of the Israeli-Palestinian peace process has been the existence of numerous informal channels of communication between individuals belonging to the two sides but not representing official positions. These are known as "track II"—as distinguished from "track I," referring to official talks. For nearly forty years, often with the impartial financial and logistical backing of Norway, Sweden, and other European countries, track II has aspired to contribute to the process by enriching each side's understanding of the other's mind-set and readiness to compromise without binding either. In some cases, where track II involved individuals who went on to play a role in official negotiations, these informal talks gave one side a better understanding of the personalities of the other side's negotiators.

The Oslo Accords began as track II conversations. I have participated in and even organized track II talks that fed vital insights to both sides' decision-making echelon in anticipation of official talks. In at least two instances of track II, the Ayalon-Nusseibeh one-page statement of principles of July 2002 and the far more detailed Geneva Accords of October 2003, high-level individuals from both sides agreed on an outline of final status, only to have their conclusions rejected at the highest level and eventually become a dead letter.

Viewed with hindsight from the vantage point of mid-2015, track II has failed. Indeed, recent years have witnessed fewer and fewer Israeli-Palestinian track II initiatives as official track I negotiating attempts have repeatedly and spectacularly collapsed, violence has decimated mutual trust, and cynicism and despair have increased on both sides. In 2000, the Camp David failure led to the bloody second intifada, while in 2008 the Olmert-Abbas failure catalyzed Abbas's virtual renunciation of negotiations and, after a brief engagement with Netanyahu essentially to please the Barack Obama administration, his resort to the international community. Without the prospect of productive track I or official negotiations, it is difficult for track II talks to convene, much less define a realistic agenda and contribute to the process.

Among West Bank Palestinians, a strong antinormalization movement has emerged in recent years that rejects even virtual track II initiatives that employ the Internet, like the *bitterlemons* channel I coedited for many years with a Palestinian colleague. In 2014, even *Haaretz* West Bank correspondent Amira Hass, who lives in Ramallah and reports sympathetically on the Palestinian dilemma, was banned by students from speaking at Bir Zeit University. And in Gaza, Hamas opposes any and all direct interaction with the other side. Among many Israelis there is a strong sense that informal talks long ago exhausted their usefulness: after all these years, there is a limit to how many times the same "usual suspects" on both sides can meet to rehash the same issues. Here and there in Israel there is also a recognition that, with few exceptions (one was Sari Nusseibeh of the forward-looking Ayalon-Nusseibeh agreement; Nusseibeh has since felt obliged to "recant" many of his progressive ideas), Palestinians needed some sort of official nod to participate and were careful about what they would agree to put down on paper, thereby limiting the innovative dimension of track II.

One way or another, if in the near term progress is to be made toward Palestinian-Israeli agreements, it will probably not be channeled through the two sides' civil societies.

ECONOMIC PEACE

One of the most persistent themes in the approach to the Palestinian issue on the part of both Israel and international interlocutors has been the notion that the road to peace has a strong economic dimension. According to this thinking, if the Palestinian economy is developing and Palestinians are feeling more prosperous and hopeful regarding their material future, either the chances for a successful peace process improve or, at a minimum, the danger of violence directed toward Israelis subsides.

Note that as far back as the Peel Commission report, the "conciliatory effect on the Palestinian Arabs of the material prosperity which Jewish immigration would bring in Palestine" was found to have failed as a catalyst for coexistence. Indeed, as early as 1923 Revisionist Zionist leader Zeev Jabotinsky recognized, "To think that the Arabs will voluntarily consent to the realization of Zionism in return for the cultural and economic benefits we can bestow on them is infantile. This childish fantasy of our 'Arabo-philes' comes from some kind of contempt for the Arab people, of some kind of unfounded view of this race as a rabble ready to be bribed in order to sell out their homeland for a railroad network."

Yet immediately after Israel occupied the West Bank and Gaza Strip in June 1967, it proceeded as if ignorant of admonitions by Peel, Jabotinsky, or anyone else. Israeli minister of defense Moshe Dayan threw open the green line border and encouraged Israelis and Palestinians to go back and forth and interact at the commercial level. Israeli agricultural experts inaugurated programs to assist Palestinian farmers, who could market their produce in Israel and, through Israel, to Europe. Legions of Palestinian day laborers came to work in Israel. Both sides prospered. Israeli security officials responsible for the Palestinian territories were certain a formula had been found to prevent violence and ensure harmony, even if a political solution was proving elusive.

It took twenty years, until the outbreak of the first intifada in December 1987, to prove them wrong and force at least a partial closing of borders and imposition of restrictions on economic interaction. Yet the emphasis on prosperity as an ingredient for peace continued. In July 2000, when I represented Prime Minister Ehud Barak in recruiting American Jewish and media support for a hoped-for breakthrough at Camp David, a key talking point was the need for Washington to provide funds for Palestinian desalination projects and for refugee compensation in order to "grease" the process.

Following two intifadas, in 2002, the international community pressured PA president Yasser Arafat to appoint a distinguished international economist, Salam Fayyad, as finance minister—from 2007 until 2013 he was also prime minister—again on the assumption that economic development and interaction with Israel, which he indeed delivered on, would help advance a peaceful settlement. In 2007, too, the Quartet (a peacemaking initiative involving the United States, European Union, United Nations, and Russia) delegated former British prime minister Tony Blair to promote economic development in the territories as a key ingredient of an eventual peaceful settlement (he resigned in 2015). In 2005, outgoing World Bank president James Wolfensohn served briefly as the Quartet's representative for promoting economic development in the Gaza Strip as Israel withdrew.

In 2009, Benjamin Netanyahu's Likud campaign in Knesset elections featured an "economic peace" platform for developing the Palestinian

Authority as a necessary prelude to peace talks. And hard-line Israeli politicians like Naftali Bennett promote ideas for developing the 40 percent of the West Bank that is under full or partial PA control (Areas A and B) as a means of ensuring peaceful interaction in the absence of a viable peace process, which they either oppose or do not believe is feasible.

Further, the international community has responded to all three mini-wars between Israel and Gaza-based Hamas since 2007 by rushing in to pledge huge sums of infrastructure aid for the strip and its population—pledges usually ignored, particularly by the Gulf Arab donors, in the ensuing follow-up—on the assumption that Gaza's severe economic plight and its war damages are a major cause of these conflicts. In May 2015 President Obama, in declaring that there was no chance for a peace process in the year ahead, nevertheless allowed that the United States would seek to create "business opportunities and jobs" in the Palestinian territories in order to build trust between the two sides. And in June 2015, the RAND Corporation issued a study describing the huge economic windfall that Israelis and Palestinians would benefit from if they just made peace and the economic losses they would incur if they did not.

The common denominator of nearly all these "economic peace" approaches is, as Jabotinsky noted, the whiff of colonialist patronization that they emit. They grossly undervalue the Palestinian national drive: the political, ideological, and Islamic currents that inform the Arab side of the conflict. This in turn points to a serious lacuna in strategic understanding on the part of both Israelis and third parties. Perhaps to drive home the point, note that both Palestinian intifadas erupted (in 1987 and 2000) at times of relative prosperity; even the Palestinian revolt against the British Mandate that broke out in 1936 began at a time when Palestine was relatively well off economically, albeit due primarily to Jewish development projects.

Of course economic prosperity is a good thing. Many Palestinians, particularly in the Gaza Strip, are extremely needy. Development projects should be encouraged, and offers of aid should not be sneered at. But this conflict does not derive from economic roots, and it is not fed by economic deprivation. It is political, with an increasingly strong element of religious extremism on both sides. And in the Israeli-Palestinian case, enhanced trust is not a corollary of prosperity.

CRUCIAL TURNING POINTS

It is undoubtedly difficult to assess and understand the true strategic import of historic turning points in any process as they are taking place. Hindsight is usually necessary to make that possible. Yet the sooner those turning points are understood, the more rational our thinking and decisions about the next direction to take.

This is particularly true regarding the past twenty-five years of the Israeli-Palestinian conflict and attempts to resolve it.

As a game changer, the Oslo Accords of 1993 were misunderstood in many circles—in Israel, among the Palestinians, and in the international community—as a point of no return, an irreversible achievement. In fact, as we have seen, many of the achievements of Oslo could be reversed—for example, by Palestinian suicide bombings and subsequent massive Israeli security intrusions into Palestinian Authority Area A. Recognition of Oslo's reversibility might have dictated a different approach to its implementation. (Indeed, in the Israeli-Palestinian context, reversibility can be applied to virtually everything, including the conclusions of this book; see chapter 11.)

The assassination of Yitzhak Rabin in late 1995 was, in retrospect, a deathblow to the peace process. It is one of those rare examples of a political assassination that achieves its objective, though whether the process would have succeeded had Rabin lived is, of course, open to discussion.

Two intifadas (1987–1992 and 2000–2004), on the other hand, were correctly understood in real time as warnings that urgent progress on the ground was needed. They helped generate the Oslo Accords and the Gaza withdrawal. Taken together with the Rabin assassination, Israel's brutal suppression of the second intifada under the leadership of Ariel Sharon, and Hamas's repeated use of force from its base in Gaza, they project a grim recognition of the efficacy of violence in altering the course of the Israeli-Palestinian conflict.

Apropos Hamas and Gaza, the unilateral Israeli withdrawal from the Gaza Strip in 2005 was at the time misinterpreted as a step toward additional withdrawals leading to an end-of-conflict agreement and as an important advance in Palestinian state-building. In fact, Prime Minister Ariel Sharon, a total skeptic regarding peace with the Arabs, apparently intended it as a one-off gesture to rebuff international pressure on the Palestinian issue (though the simultaneous removal of four small settlements from the northern West Bank was seemingly intended to suggest that additional West Bank withdrawals were possible—an idea pursued abortively by Sharon's successor, Ehud Olmert).

Indeed, the outcome was even less progressive than Sharon himself seemingly aimed for. The Palestinian state-building enterprise in Gaza was a total failure. Hamas took over the Gaza Strip and has been attacking Israel intermittently ever since. Consequently, most Israelis understand the outcome of the Gaza withdrawal as a warning regarding the possible consequences of any further withdrawal from even part of the West Bank.

The collapse of the Olmert-Abbas Annapolis track in September 2008 has seemingly not yet been fully understood as a major turning point for the Palestinians. Olmert offered Abbas the farthest-reaching Israeli territorial withdrawal yet from the West Bank, as well as a capital in East Jerusalem, reasonable security provisions, a formula for symbolic refugee return to Israel, and an international consortium to administer the Jerusalem Holy Basin (the Old City, Temple Mount, City of David, and Mount of Olives) in which three Arab Muslim countries, including Palestine, have a majority.

Abbas turned the offer down ("the gaps were wide"). Ever since, he has shunned or downplayed direct negotiations and instead resorted to the international community for Palestinian state recognition, for condemnation of Israel for alleged crimes against humanity, and for delegitimization of Israel through the boycott, divestment, and sanctions campaign. Abbas pays little more than lip service to the Arab League and Arab Peace Initiative. As former head of Israel Defense Forces Intelligence Shlomo Gazit points out, it is as if Abbas, mimicking Israel's "periphery doctrine" of the country's early decades, when it sought alliances with Iran and Turkey to balance Egyptian leader Gamal Abdel Nasser's aggressive Arab nationalism closer to home, has abandoned the Middle East core in favor of a solution from the international "periphery."

Here a case can be made that Israeli governmental instability also created negative turning points for the Palestinians. In 1995 Rabin's assassination, followed within half a year by the Israeli elections that first brought Netanyahu to power, radically altered the equilibrium of negotiations. In 2000, Arafat was dealing with Barak's lame-duck government, which had lost its majority and was heading for elections. And in 2008, Abbas knew during his conversations with Olmert that the Israeli prime minister would not remain in office. Do these events—essentially, the vicissitudes of Israeli politics—justify or at least partially explain Arafat's behavior at Camp David or Abbas walking away from Olmert's far-reaching peace offer?

Then there is the virtual collapse of the post-Ottoman Middle East state system. Beginning spectacularly in 2011 with a series of revolutions in dysfunctional and often fragmented countries, it was initially misunderstood in some Arab, Turkish, and Western circles as a regional move toward democratization, perhaps with a moderate Islamist slant. Since Israeli hawks like Netanyahu and Natan Sharansky had projected Arab democratization as a precondition for peace with the Palestinians, this appeared initially to be a cause for optimism in the Palestinian context. But the Arab reality quickly deteriorated into civil war, terrorism, and in many cases the incarceration of moderate reformers.

While revolution did not reach either the West Bank or the Gaza Strip, many Israelis understood the entire dynamic quickly and intuitively as a warning not to proceed with the establishment of a Palestinian state. Why, in this atmosphere of collapsing dysfunctional Arab states, create yet another one?

GOD AND THE CONFLICT

Does invoking God's will help or hinder a solution? The accumulated evidence appears to indicate that progress is best served by keeping God out of the conflict. But this is difficult in view of the nature of both Orthodox Judaism and Islam as all-inclusive prescriptions for every aspect of life. Certainly the mainstream West Bank settler movement and all the Palestinian Islamist movements, such as Hamas, broadly base their views and positions on their understanding of God's will. So, presumably, do avowedly Islamist state actors like Saudi Arabia. Even one active Christian American mediator, President George W. Bush, allegedly told Palestinian negotiators in 2005 that God had told him to "get the Palestinians their state and get the Israelis their security."

To be sure, a relative handful of moderate Jewish and Palestinian religious officials have at times met and tried, admirably, to reconcile their religious and political views. Their failures are no more disappointing than those of secular politicians, diplomats, and security officials. Currently, both Sunni and Shiite Islamists are increasingly overwhelming the entire Middle East, and fundamentalist Jewish persons and views increasingly influence Israel's position regarding the West Bank and East Jerusalem. It would appear that God is a growing part of the Israeli-Palestinian conflict—to its detriment.

Here is what a well-known Israeli humorist and Old Testament expert, Meir Shalev, had to say on the issue in mid-October 2015 in *Yedioth Ahronoth*. Noting the trail of blood and mayhem left in history by the three monotheistic religions, Shalev commented, "A meeting of religious officials in the cause of ceasing bloodshed in the Holy Land . . . is reminiscent of a festive gathering of Jack the Ripper, Charles Manson and the Boston Strangler for a discussion of the sanctity of life."

LEADERSHIP

Neither Palestinians nor Israelis have enjoyed the kind of consistent leadership needed to shepherd the Israeli-Palestinian peace process as projected by Oslo: a series of incremental agreements to be reached and implemented over years. On the Israeli side, I have already noted the abrupt and tragic removal from the scene of Yitzhak Rabin, the crude negotiating errors made by Barak and Olmert, and the cynicism of Ariel Sharon. Benjamin Netanyahu has never projected a serious approach concerning peace with the Palestinians or had a viable strategy for dealing with them, whether in the West Bank or in Gaza. The absence of a detailed and viable Netanyahu peace plan (see chapters 9 and 10) is one example. The summer 2014 war with Hamas in Gaza, fought in the total absence of a strategy for winning or even merely coming to terms with Hamas, is another (see chapter 5).

Moreover, the very structure of Israel's political system renders it nearly impossible to translate the public's essential support for a two-state solution into something concrete. After all, a majority of Israelis repeatedly endorses a two-state outcome; yet a majority repeatedly returns the nationalist pro-settler Right to power, and even when a "security dove" like Yitzhak Rabin or Ehud Barak is elected, political realities and coalition constraints thwart a conclusive process. In this sense, the 1977–1981 Israeli-Egyptian peace process was extremely fortunate in being shepherded to fruition by strong leaders like Anwar Sadat and Menachem Begin, the latter enjoying a uniquely large Knesset majority. (The Israeli-Jordanian peace of 1994 required virtually no territorial concessions and no removal of settlements on Israel's part. Hence it was easy for the public to support.)

On the Palestinian side, in retrospect it appears that the death of Yasser Arafat removed the only leader capable of garnering even a shaky consensus for a two-state agreement among Palestinian national and Islamist movements, many of which, like Arafat himself, were violent in nature and launched or condoned terrorism to achieve their objectives against Israel. Arafat, had he wished to cease violence, enhance his credibility, and reach an agreement, might have been able to deliver.

Today, many Palestinians are prepared to acknowledge that Arafat saw terrorist violence against Israeli civilians as a legitimate weapon even at the height of negotiations. Equally problematic was the credibility issue. Unfortunately, the Israeli leadership was all too ready to overlook this extreme character fault—which was far more obvious at the time than Arafat's secret condoning of violence—in the interests of keeping negotiations moving.

Twice when I brought high-level American visitors to meet Arafat in the mid-1990s, I personally experienced Arafat's primitive displays of mendacity. In a meeting at the Muqataa (PA headquarters) in Ramallah, the leader of a major American Jewish organization cited specific instances of anti-Semitic incitement by Palestinian schoolteachers that were broadcast by CNN. Arafat, in response, feigned horror: "This is terrible. I didn't know. I'll deal with it immediately." Even his close aides smirked. A few weeks later PLO activist Hanan Ashrawi, who had been present, took me aside at another meeting and allowed, "We have to organize these meetings with Arafat a bit better." I never quite understood what she meant . . .

On a second occasion, at his headquarters in Gaza City, several US congresspersons asked Arafat about a particularly bloody Palestinian terrorist attack at Bet Lid in central Israel a few days earlier in January 1995. Arafat responded by displaying a set of counterfeit Israeli ID cards of truly primitive quality (he let me examine them) and claiming that they were authentic originals and that they somehow proved the Mossad was behind the attack, which was intended to make him look bad. Here the embarrassed apology came as we were departing, whispered by then PLO "foreign minister" Nabil Shaat.

Arafat was Israel's first Palestinian peace partner. He was succeeded by Mahmoud Abbas, a genuine opponent of the use of violence for political means but a weak leader who lost control over the Gaza Strip and was unable to make the painful concessions necessary to reach an end-of-conflict agreement or to "deliver" his diaspora constituency regarding those concessions. One way or another, both Arafat's penchant for violence and duplicity and Abbas's leadership weakness have constituted major obstacles to successful final-status negotiations.

ONLY FAILURES AND OBSTACLES?

This litany of failures and misjudgments on the part of Israelis, Palestinians, and third parties should not be understood to mean they have done nothing right. On the contrary, for more than two decades, committed and highly professional negotiators from both sides have displayed a great deal of ingenuity and intelligence in trying to move the process forward. While the Oslo Accords and the Palestinian Authority have their faults, they were almost certainly the best that could be done in their day. Even at the time of this writing, security cooperation in the West Bank and coordination of even limited aid and passage to the Gaza Strip represent huge achievements for very dedicated people on both sides of the separation fences. And those informal, or track II, projects that, despite the odds, continue to bring together "civilians" from both sides are keeping alive a flame of positive coexistence and cooperation.

In view of these achievements, some would still argue that the Oslo process has not (or at least not yet) run its course.

ATTEMPTS AT THE SUMMIT TO NEGOTIATE FINAL STATUS IN 2000 AND 2008: NOT ENOUGH OR TOO MUCH?

The leaders of both sides of the conflict have made two concerted attempts at the highest level to sit down together and generate a two-state solution. Both attempts were based on the Oslo formula, or "menu," of final-status issues to be discussed following a period of autonomy. Both failed spectacularly, with the 2000 Camp David summit quickly leading to the second intifada and the 2008 Olmert-Abbas meetings persuading Abbas to pursue an "international" solution.

Are two such high-level attempts sufficient to justify a conclusion that the Oslo paradigm has run its course and that a different approach must be invoked? Is this a good example of what Albert Einstein meant when he allegedly defined insanity as doing the same thing over and over again and expecting a different result? Or are two attempts a mere beginning, to be followed up by more peacemaking efforts based on the same model?

Gilead Sher, who negotiated with the Palestinians on behalf of Prime Minister Ehud Barak in 1999 and 2000 and has studied the issues ever since, endorsed the second possibility in a talk in January 2015, when he noted that, out of more than twenty years of effort since Oslo, only two attempts were devoted to a final-status agreement. In a similar vein, US negotiator Martin Indyk stated in May 2014, in summing up Secretary of State John Kerry's failed nine-month peacemaking attempt of 2013 and 2014, "The reality is that aside from Camp David and Annapolis [the Olmert-Abbas talks of 2008], serious permanent status talks have been a rarity since the signing of the Oslo Accords in 1993. For all of its flaws, this makes the past nine months important."

Whether they were important in a positive or a negative sense is the topic of the next chapter.

SEVEN

Lessons from Kerry's Failure and the American Role

US Secretary of State John Kerry's 2013–2014 attempt to galvanize an Israeli-Palestinian peace process illustrates clearly what has been wrong with the Oslo process—on all sides—since its inception.

The years between the failure of the Olmert-Abbas negotiations (Annapolis initiative) in late 2008 and the advent of Kerry's new Oslo-based final-status initiative in July 2013 were virtually bereft of Israeli-Palestinian peace talks. Prime Minister Ehud Olmert was replaced in 2009 by Benjamin Netanyahu; President George W. Bush by Barack Obama. The latter appointed a peace emissary, George Mitchell, and pressured Netanyahu into applying a limited freeze on settlement construction for the better part of a year in order to encourage Israeli-Palestinian talks. Netanyahu also reluctantly agreed to endorse the idea of a two-state solution in a public address, the June 2009 Bar Ilan speech. But beyond a single unsuccessful meeting between Netanyahu and Mahmoud Abbas, little happened bilaterally: Netanyahu put together successive coalitions clearly oriented toward expanding the settlements. Abbas turned his attention to the United Nations, where he sought recognition for a Palestinian state.

By now it should have been clear that the Oslo formula for trying to agree on all final-status issues was not working. Abbas had turned down Olmert's far-reaching offer; he knew that Netanyahu would be nowhere near as generous. Abbas's UN initiative appeared to point to Palestinian readiness to entertain a more limited formula for achieving statehood without an end-of-conflict agreement. But in the absence of close Israeli-Palestinian consultation, Abbas's motives were suspect in Israeli eyes. Then, too, the United States, prodded by Israel, remained adamantly opposed to this sort of "internationalization" of the issue and bypassing of direct negotiations, while Netanyahu insisted that in return for a Palestinian state, he needed Palestinian agreement on pre-1967 narrative issues such as recognition of a Jewish state and abandonment of the right of return.

Kerry, who became secretary of state in the second Obama administration in January 2013, was an adherent of the "parameters of a final-status agreement are well known" school and clearly believed strongly in his own powers of persuasion. Not only did he set out once again to implement the Oslo final-status provisions, but, even after he acknowledged failure to bring about a two-state solution to the Israeli-Palestinian conflict in March–April 2014, we witnessed a flood of learned diagnoses of the reasons that were nearly all topical, focusing on the apparent immediate catalysts of failure rather than reassessing the actual Oslo process and its underpinnings.

Thus, Palestinians blamed continued Israeli settlement-building initiatives and Israel's refusal to release a fourth and final cohort of veteran Palestinian prisoners, as agreed under Kerry's prodding. A US assessment published by senior Israeli journalist Nahum Barnea and unofficially attributed to Martin Indyk pointed to the settlements as the primary obstacle to progress. Indeed, if Netanyahu did not intend settlement construction to send a direct signal of his real intent toward the Palestinians, at a minimum it represented an essential commitment to his broadly antipeace coalition.

In contrast, sources close to the government of Israel accused Palestinian leader Mahmoud Abbas of repeatedly inventing justifications to delay negotiating or to provoke Israeli delays (e.g., new conditions and demands regarding territory and prisoners, applications to join UN conventions, unity talks with Hamas, threats to dismantle the Palestinian Authority, and so forth). Indeed, none of these Palestinian initiatives taken during negotiations was helpful or reflected a relationship of trust. A document of uncertain authenticity circulated by the Israel Prime Minister's Office and allegedly drafted by chief Palestinian negotiator Saeb Erekat purported to lay out a deliberate Palestinian plan for delays and obfuscation during the closing stages of the talks. And Abbas walked away from a critical meeting with President Obama in March without responding to a set of American proposals, then, upon his return to Ramallah, rejected them publicly.

Both Kerry and Indyk emphasized after the fact that a sense of urgency to avert the catastrophe of a binational state had motivated them; yet that urgency had been nowhere evident in Jerusalem and Ramallah.

Apparently, here and there Kerry registered a modicum of deniable progress. Thus, Netanyahu reportedly agreed to the 1967 borders with land swaps, though he still defined the settlement blocs in an exorbitant way; softened his demands on the Jewish state issue; and allowed that 1948 refugees could apply to return to Israel on an individual basis—this last concession was presumably a reaffirmation of a family-reunification mechanism that flourished between 1948 and 1967. The Palestinians reportedly demonstrated flexibility on refugee numbers and agreed to tolerate construction in the settlement blocs. Netanyahu cleverly (in contrast with Abbas) responded to American proposals with conditional nonrejections. Word was leaked of a London-based back channel between attorney Yitzhak Molcho, representing Netanyahu, and Hussein Agha, ostensibly representing Abbas: the two allegedly agreed on a formula for borders and refugees. Both Abbas and Netanyahu later repudiated the formula and denied authorizing the channel, which had actually existed for fully five years, and had never catalyzed a peace breakthrough, but provided both leaders with "cover" to rebuff pressures for a more serious process.

All these revelations followed upon nine months of effort that were managed, as usual, under the slogan "nothing is agreed until everything is agreed," meaning that in fact, when the talks ended, nothing—conveniently for both Netanyahu and Abbas—could be considered by their political enemies at home to have been agreed. Particularly disturbing was the fact that by the time of its collapse, the "process" that had now ended or been suspended had morphed into a framework for maintaining largely unproductive proximity talks between the United States and each of the two negotiating sides, Israel and the Palestine Liberation Organization (PLO). There were no productive face-to-face talks, with the possible exception of the deniable secret back-channel contacts. By the end of April 2014, when the nine months allotted by Kerry himself for the process elapsed, the very idea (which in any case proved abortive) of continuation or extension of the talks appeared to be little more than a formula for ensuring relative quiet and stability on the Israeli-Palestinian scene for a few more months rather than progress toward two states.

Ostensibly, all three relevant parties were still interested in achieving a two-state solution. In reality, they sought little more than quiet and stability in the short term. The Obama administration wished to boast of an ongoing process as it approached midterm elections in November 2014. Netanyahu sought to leverage the mere existence of a peace process into relative success in blunting international efforts to impose a political and economic boycott on Israel, all the while proceeding with settlement activity. And for Abbas the complete absence of talks could, particularly if blamed convincingly on him, have resulted in catastrophic financial penalties for the Palestinian Authority on the part of the United States and European Union.

Yet, beyond the superficial level reflected in all these postmortems, it was easy enough to identify the constant factors of real substance that, because they were ignored once again, caused this latest initiative to end so ingloriously.

The most glaring lacuna evident in the Kerry team's preparations for this latest round of talks was its apparent failure to examine why the Oslo formula had not produced a two-state solution in the course of the twenty years leading up to 2013 and 2014. A cursory analysis should have demonstrated what we discussed in the previous chapter: that the formula laid out by the Oslo Declaration of Principles (DOP) in September 1993—all-or-nothing negotiations between Israel and the PLO over a set menu of all final-status issues—virtually guaranteed failure in 2000 (Camp David) and 2008 (the Olmert-Abbas negotiations), when the Israeli and Palestinian leaderships were ostensibly much more inclined to reach agreement than were Abbas and Netanyahu in 2013 and 2014. So dispiriting had those failures been for both sides that from late 2008 until July 2013 no serious talks had even taken place.

Indeed, it should have been understood that repeated collapses of the Oslo final-status process are in some ways worse than no negotiations at all. Failure, after all, discredits the idea of a negotiated solution in the eyes of both Israelis and Palestinians. It also empowers extremists. Thus, one can make the case that Kerry's spring 2014 failure led Abbas to overcome his hesitations and declare the formation of a unity government with Gaza-based Hamas, giving the extremist Islamist organization a freer hand in the West Bank. Shortly thereafter, Hamas activists from Hebron kidnapped and murdered three Israeli yeshiva students near Efrat in the West Bank, setting into motion an escalatory series of atrocities and provocations that culminated in the summer 2014 war between Israel and Hamas.

Yet Kerry and his team proceeded uncritically to adopt the very same Oslo paradigm for yet another try. It is difficult to comprehend why he embraced this approach. How, for example, could the senior US official cited by Barnea after the failure express surprise that persistent settlement construction by the Netanyahu government (which Kerry agreed in advance could continue) sabotaged the talks, when this had been a key negative factor in the eyes of all peace-minded parties for years, even preceding Oslo? Kerry knew he could not extract from Netanyahu a settlement freeze in 2013. Yet he initiated the process anyway.

An analysis of the Oslo final-status formula and its repeated failures points to several lessons that the Kerry team ignored at its peril. Following on our earlier discussion of factors relevant to previous abortive negotiations, by 2013 and 2014 they should have been obvious.

LESSON 1: SEPARATE AND SET ASIDE PRE-1967 ISSUES

One lesson concerns the menu of final-status issues. The Oslo DOP calls on Israel and the PLO to discuss "Jerusalem, refugees, settlements, security arrangements, borders, relations and cooperation with other neighbors, and other issues of common interest" — an obviously incomplete list that led negotiators quickly to fill in the lacuna with topics like holy places. The combination of mandatory negotiating topics and a perceived ("nothing is agreed . . .") need to agree on everything soon presented problems that have proven insurmountable ever since and can clearly be seen to have dogged Kerry's effort.

As noted earlier, the DOP failed to distinguish between two very different sorts of topics for negotiations: pre-1967, or narrative, issues and post-1967 issues. The former refer to refugees and the right of return (a 1948 issue), holy places (an issue as old as Judaism and Islam), and anything touching on Israel's essential nature and the status of Israel's Palestinian Arab population. The latter refer to the issues created by Israel's occupation since the 1967 Six-Day War: borders, sovereignty, security, and a Palestinian capital in Jerusalem. Relatively speaking, the latter are mundane state-to-state negotiating topics that are far more easily managed than the former, which are virtually "existential" in the eyes of the parties.

In a similar vein, Kerry's team claims that it made progress in closing the territorial gap and persuading Abbas to accept an Israeli security presence in the Jordan Valley for at least five years. But these "post-1967" achievements could hardly be trumpeted in real time by Kerry, or even implemented, because they were held hostage to total nonagreement on narrative issues. As far as we know, negotiations sponsored by Kerry during 2013 and 2014 failed to narrow those pre-1967 differences.

This striking dichotomy suggests that a viable two-state effort based on lessons learned would separate out pre- and post-1967 issues and concentrate only on the latter by insisting that the nonnarrative issues be discussed and agreed first as a separate package. Remarks by President Obama in May 2011 seemed to hint at such an approach when he suggested dealing first with borders and security. While an agreement on these issues that is not conditioned on a resolution of all final-status issues would not end the conflict or all claims, it would, if successful, place the conflict on a far more manageable state-to-state basis in terms of which the intractable narrative issues could be temporarily or even indefinitely postponed.

Yet Kerry's team, echoed by chief Israeli negotiator Tzipi Livni, insisted that all final-status issues would be on the table simultaneously, and all would have to be agreed. Worse, Kerry himself appears to have mixed up the issues and allowed the two sides to do so as well in ways that guaranteed deadlock. Thus, Kerry placed Netanyahu's Jewish state demand front and center on the list of issues the United States agreed to and that Abbas would have to accept, even lobbying prominent Arab leaders to prod Abbas. He ignored the fact that, for Abbas, this would be political suicide, if not a death warrant: virtually no Palestinian is prepared to acquiesce to this self-definition of Israel, and Abbas would be denying the most fundamental Palestinian narrative if he did.

That narrative, we recall, holds that Jews are not a people with a right to a sovereign state, that what they call the Land of Israel is not their historic homeland, that they were party to a colonialist plot that denied the land to Palestinians in 1948, and that accordingly the state of Israel was born in sin. The PLO, on behalf of the Palestinian people, is prepared, in the spirit of compromise, to recognize the state of Israel (not the Jewish state of Israel) within the 1967 lines and allow it to define itself as it wishes.

Simultaneously, Kerry and Netanyahu accepted a list of veteran Palestinian prisoners to be released by Israel as a confidence-building gesture that included, in the fourth and final tranche scheduled for the end of the nine-month period, fourteen Arab citizens of Israel convicted of terrorist crimes prior to the advent of the Oslo process in 1993. Their inclusion implied that Abbas somehow had jurisdiction over Palestinian citizens of Israel, thereby calling into question the Palestinian commitment ostensibly to accept the sovereignty of the state of Israel (even if not a Jewish state) as constituted in 1948. In April 2014, when Netanyahu apparently belatedly realized the meaning of this concession on his part, he balked and backed out of his commitment.

LESSON 2: REPOSITION NEGOTIATIONS AS STATE TO STATE RATHER THAN STATE TO LIBERATION MOVEMENT

The Oslo DOP was an agreement between a sovereign state, Israel, and a 1960s-style Third World liberation movement, the Palestine Liberation Organization. Obviously, in 1993 there was no alternative formula for launching an Israeli-Palestinian peace process. As we saw earlier, this approach worked well enough as a paradigm for creating an autonomous Palestinian entity in the West Bank and Gaza Strip insofar as the issues in question—a finite Palestinian territory and population—touched only on the Palestinian populations of those territories.

But when negotiations turned to the issues of final status, Israel confronted an organization that, as we have noted, represented not merely the population of the Palestinian Authority but all Palestinians everywhere, meaning principally the five-million-strong refugee diaspora, and even, as we have seen, aspired to represent Palestinian citizens of Israel. This imbalance has proven crucial in thwarting progress. Here again, had a new negotiating paradigm insisted on first concluding a separate deal on the outlines of a state and set aside the narrative issues, like the right of return, that dominate Palestinian diaspora thinking, it might have been possible to reposition the conflict on a more productive state-to-state basis in terms of which Abbas would approach talks with Israel as president of the state of Palestine rather than as head of a diaspora-heavy liberation movement.

LESSON 3: TAKE THE REAL MEASURE OF THE ISRAELI AND PALESTINIAN LEADERS

A striking characteristic of the Kerry-led process was the degree of optimism that the US secretary of state managed to generate in the early stages. It was infectious: the many Israeli and Palestinian experts whom the Kerry team contacted to commission detailed opinion polls and discuss issues like Jordan Valley security came away convinced of progress, even when the mediators in fact had little to show for their efforts.

This may have been a calculated tactic for improving the atmosphere, but Kerry may also have been carried away by the encouraging feedback he received from Abbas and Netanyahu. Obviously, neither leader wished to be accused of sabotaging a US-led initiative. Yet the most superficial observation regarding not what the leaders say but what they do and what ideologies they represent should readily have deflated this American balloon.

Netanyahu, while ostensibly pledged to a two-state solution, established a governing coalition in March 2013 that leaned heavily on settler and pro-settler elements, including many in his own Likud party, who were awarded the necessary portfolios for advancing their cause. In speeches in Israel, he constantly excoriated the Palestinians as enemies and even went so far as to link them to Nazi extermination efforts: hardly an attempt to ready the public for peace. A large liberal party brought into the coalition, Yesh Atid, focused on middle-class socioeconomic demands and had little interest in the Palestinian issue. The small HaTnua party, led by Tzipi Livni, was the only active advocate within the coalition of a two-state solution.

Thus, by definition, this was not a peace government. Before, during, and after Kerry's initiative, members of Netanyahu's own coalition repeatedly presented to the Knesset ultranationalist legislative initiatives: annexing the Jordan Valley, mandating parliamentary approval for even entering into talks about Jerusalem and the refugee issue, mandating a referendum if sovereign Israeli territory (East Jerusalem, whose 1967 annexation under Israeli law is not recognized internationally) is to be handed over to a peace partner, and relegating Israeli Arabs to second-class status. Though most were never enacted, all had the cumulative effect, sanctioned by the prime minister, of reducing both Israeli and Palestinian support for the process.

Nor, throughout the nine months of negotiations, was there any indication whatsoever that Netanyahu would, whether to enable progress, signal goodwill, or implement an agreement of any sort, disband his settlement-building coalition in favor of an alternative center-left coalition that would be more attuned to compromise solutions along lines entertained in previous Oslo-based negotiations by Yitzhak Rabin, Shimon Peres, Ehud Barak, and Ehud Olmert. Indeed, virtually unimpeded by the prime minister, the settler elements in the government proceeded to launch provocative new construction initiatives at every critical juncture in the talks.

If Netanyahu, backed by a coalition of his choosing, was not a partner, neither was Abbas. The Palestinian leader had generally avoided committing to serious negotiations ever since walking away from his talks with Prime Minister Ehud Olmert in September 2008. Even when the first Obama administration persuaded Olmert's successor, Netanyahu, to implement an unprecedented (though incomplete) ten-month Israeli settlement freeze in 2009, Abbas stalled and avoided negotiating until the last minute. One obvious reason is that he knew that Netanyahu would never come close to the far-reaching proposals tabled earlier by Olmert just prior to his resignation. Abbas had first ignored then rejected these proposals, albeit under the mitigating circumstance of Olmert's lame-duck status, because, as we saw earlier, they still did not come close to satisfying the narrative demands that he and his constituency had cultivated and sanctified.

Netanyahu, by the way, could offer to renew negotiations with Abbas "without preconditions," thereby signaling to Abbas that what had been discussed and perhaps tentatively agreed with Olmert was null and void, precisely because of the "nothing is agreed until everything is agreed" principle. When, toward the end of the freeze, Abbas was persuaded to sit down with Netanyahu, one session proved sufficient to justify, from his point of view, his avoidance of negotiations.

Further, from a domestic Palestinian standpoint, Abbas's capacity to speak for all Palestinians was constrained. He did not rule the Gaza Strip, even though that territory was on the negotiating table. Indeed, Gaza was ruled by Hamas, which rejects the entire Oslo-based two-state solution. Then, too, Abbas's electoral mandate had long since expired, while former Gaza security chief and Arafat lieutenant Mohammed Dahlan was energetically challenging his leadership of Fatah.

It is not surprising that Netanyahu and Abbas apparently never once met during Kerry's nine-month negotiation process. It is surprising that Kerry thought he had viable negotiating partners.

LESSON 4: FACTOR IN WHAT IS HAPPENING IN THE REGION AND IN WASHINGTON

Both Netanyahu and Abbas, it must be added, were also dealing with the problematic regional situation ignited by the so-called Arab Spring.

When the process began, the Arab world had been in chaos for more than two years. Islamist elements that reject Israel's existence outright were becoming an increasingly powerful factor in the region.

While Kerry could argue that the absence of war threats against Israel provided a congenial setting for both leaders to offer concessions at relatively low cost, they could be forgiven for adopting a less innovative "keep your powder dry," sit-tight attitude. Not surprisingly, Kerry proved unable to recruit any sort of serious and sustained regional Arab support for his end-of-conflict efforts. After all, he confronted an Arab world preoccupied by severe internal strife clearly unrelated to the Palestinian issue. Indeed, on some vital security issues at least two Arab states were in need of close coordination with Israel, regardless of the status of the peace process—Egypt concerning Sinai and Gaza; Jordan concerning southern Syria—while rumors abounded of Israeli intelligence contacts with Saudi Arabia and the United Arab Emirates as well.

True, Kerry was able to recruit some pan-Arab support for the process with reference to the 2002 Arab Peace Initiative (API). Yet the very same Arab world that approved the API in 2002 was now in tatters.

Arguably, the overall fabric of differences separating the positions of Netanyahu and Abbas was unbridgeable. Certainly, a US mediator who nevertheless aspired to register progress should have been prepared to twist arms and exercise heavy pressure on either or both sides, with the active backing of the White House. Yet, with the exception of abortive European Union threats, quietly sanctioned by Washington, to impose economic punishment on both sides (cutting off support for the Palestinian Authority if the Palestinian side caused the process to fail; tightening sanctions regarding Israel's settlements), no such pressure was apparently forthcoming.

Further, Netanyahu and Abbas both presumably recognized that President Obama was less enthusiastic about Kerry's process than Kerry himself and that the White House and the State Department were not always fully coordinated. Inevitably, the Israeli and Palestinian leaders were also aware that the United States was dramatically altering—and lowering—its strategic profile elsewhere in the Middle East, thereby weakening Washington's capacity to twist their arms.

To wit, Obama supported first the removal from power in Egypt of Hosni Mubarak, seen by the Netanyahu government as a relatively friendly Arab leader, and then a move to hold free elections that brought the Muslim Brotherhood—the parent organization of Gaza-based Hamas—to power in Cairo. Washington next spearheaded a "leading from behind" NATO campaign against the Muammar Gadhafi regime in Libya that left that country badly fragmented, exporting terrorists and their weaponry southward into Africa, west to Tunisia, and east to Egypt and as far as Gaza/Sinai.

In September 2013, Obama backed off from an explicit threat to punish the embattled Assad regime in Syria for its use of chemical weapons, thereby seriously losing credibility in Israel and the Arab world. The American withdrawal from Iraq left behind an American-trained army that, from June 2014 on, proved incapable of withstanding the onslaught of Islamic State Sunni salafist militias bent on dismantling both Syria and Iraq. Finally, US-led nuclear negotiations with Iran and tacit cooperation with Tehran in Iraq and Syria sowed serious doubts in Jerusalem (and Riyadh and elsewhere in the Arab world) regarding American resolve to combat a perceived Iranian hegemonic drive among Shiites and related sects in the Levant and in Bahrain and Yemen on the Saudi periphery.

All these developments seemingly confirmed Israeli doubts regarding the reliability of Kerry's commitments in 2013 and 2014 to bolster Israeli security under the terms of withdrawal from the West Bank. Could Israel put its faith in the promise of a US peacekeeping force in the Jordan Valley as part of a Palestinian state solution when American public opinion overwhelmingly demanded withdrawal of the US military from the Middle East and when those forces left in place were instructed to stay out of harm's way? Could Israel depend on US training of Palestinian security forces in the aftermath of Washington's colossal failure to create a viable army in Iraq? Could US commitments to come to Israel's aid in a security crisis be trusted after Obama had backed off from his self-declared "red line" in Syria in 2013?

Not far from the Middle East, the Obama administration abandoned a 1994 commitment to Ukraine and allowed Russia in 2014 to gobble up Crimea. Along with the impending withdrawal from Afghanistan and the controversial nuclear deal with Iran, these US policies too sent a signal throughout the Middle East that, however compelling in domestic US terms Washington's reasons were for lowering its Middle East profile, in regional terms it was conceding defeat. It could not compel already reluctant Israeli and Palestinian peace partners to comply with its wishes, and it lacked the capacity to persuade doubt-ridden Israelis that they could rely on the United States to bolster and guarantee a peace agreement with the Palestinians.

LESSON 5: SET REALISTIC OBJECTIVES

Kerry launched the process in July 2013 with the announcement that his objective was an end-of-conflict, end-of-claims agreement within nine months. Seen against the course of previous final-status negotiations held in 2000 and 2008 under far more favorable circumstances, this was a highly unrealistic timetable. Even a more limited and constructive "post-1967" two-state agreement probably could not have been achieved in this time frame.

Once this became clear to Kerry, he began publicly hedging his bets, almost by the month: first, he allowed that only a framework agreement would be reached in the time allotted and not an end-of-conflict agreement; then he proposed a framework nonagreement; and, finally, he spoke of a mere agreement to keep talking. Every step backward further diminished US credibility.

THE US ROLE OVER THE YEARS

Our discussion of Kerry's peace initiative—at the time of this writing, the most recent foray by Washington into the Israeli-Palestinian conflict—brings us to a broader look at the US role. Two features stand out. First, historically, Washington has never been able to catalyze an Arab-Israel peace process on its own. Second, neither Washington nor any alternative interlocutor can, under present or conceivable near-term circumstances, bring the Israeli-Palestinian process to a comprehensive conclusion. The area where the United States might conceivably make a fruitful contribution that serves its own strategic interests, and where it has done so successfully in the past, lies somewhere in between.

The United States has never actually sponsored the contacts that led directly to a peace breakthrough between Israel and an Arab neighbor. Anwar Sadat's trip to Jerusalem in November 1977, the Oslo Accords of September 1993, and the Israel-Jordan peace treaty of October 1994 were all the products of preliminary bilateral Arab-Israel contacts that did not fully involve Washington. On the other hand, in all these cases the parties involved immediately followed up on their breakthrough by requesting massive American involvement in the ensuing negotiating process. In another important instance, in late 1991 the United States was the primary convener of the Madrid conference that produced several fruitful bilateral and multilateral channels.

Over the years, the heavy US commitment has included financial incentives and security aid to the parties, side letter commitments to Israel, numerous investigative missions, and President George W. Bush's "roadmap." Incidentally, the latter—a 2002 document outlining a series of benchmarks for bilateral progress toward final status—offers a compelling example of how Washington negotiated a mechanism for managing the process, then failed to enforce it in the face of a unilaterally issued Israeli set of fourteen reservations followed by repeated violations by both sides: hardly a confidence builder.

In the Palestinian context, Washington has sponsored and accompanied bilateral Israeli-Palestinian "Oslo talks" since 1993. These produced sustained, US-sponsored negotiations at the highest level on two occasions (Camp David, July 2000; Olmert-Abbas, 2007–2008) and several interim agreements but no final two-state solution. The George W. Bush administration helped to facilitate Israel's unilateral withdrawal from the Gaza Strip and northern West Bank in 2005. Bush also expanded the American third-party facilitator role into the Quartet (involving Russia, the United Nations, and the European Union in addition to the United States), though without any appreciable results in terms of negotiated breakthroughs.

The most advanced instances of Washington's specific involvement in Israeli-Palestinian peacemaking were the Clinton parameters of late 2000 and the George W. Bush–Condoleezza Rice sponsorship of the Olmert-Abbas talks that led to Prime Minister Ehud Olmert's far-reaching final-status offer of September 2008. Both endeavors sought to engage all final-status issues based on the "nothing is agreed until everything is agreed" credo that has been a consistent feature of Oslo-based negotiations. Both failed. The 2013–2014 Kerry initiative produced nothing nearly as advanced as these two undertakings.

In 2009, the incoming administration of President Barack Obama set out quickly to make its mark on Israeli-Palestinian negotiations by appointing a presidential emissary, George Mitchell, demanding a settlement freeze to enhance the atmosphere for negotiations, and pressuring Netanyahu to accept in principle the two-state solution. For his part, Abbas initially appeared to believe, mistakenly, that Obama would "deliver" Israel with no further need for Palestinian concessions. This reflected the generally poor understanding of the Washington policymaking dynamic that has consistently characterized the PLO leadership. In mid-2012 Abbas was again assuring interlocutors, without apparent foundation, that a second Obama administration would "deliver" Israel.

Meanwhile, the Islamist direction of Arab revolutions and a failure to reconcile with Hamas in Gaza left Abbas and the PLO leadership groping for constructive policy initiatives. The most provocative of these was the attempt, beginning in 2011, to achieve United Nations recognition of a Palestinian state. It was badly mismanaged by the Palestinians and their Arab allies and totally rejected by the Obama administration. True, Abbas's approach generated growing international support and nurtured the boycott, divestment, and sanctions movement. But these achievements had no positive effect on the situation on the ground in Palestine.

In contrast to Abbas, Netanyahu has displayed considerable manipulative skill vis-à-vis the Obama administration in obfuscating the peace process while expanding Israel's West Bank presence. In 2009 he accepted a limited settlement freeze and endorsed, pro forma, the two-state solution. But at the same time, he finessed and even ignored administration demands while relying on congressional, American Jewish, and evangelical support and shifting attention away from the Palestinian issue toward the threat from Iran and the overflow of Arab revolutions. All the while, Netanyahu succeeded in maintaining a large measure of security and economic cooperation with the Palestinian Authority while nevertheless thickening and spreading the settlements and advancing the Jewish demographic encirclement of Arab East Jerusalem at an alarming pace. In 2015 he reportedly imposed another, unannounced freeze on new settlement construction, apparently due to concern over unacceptable diplomatic friction with the United States and the European Union. Ultimately, and notably, many of these achievements either went up in smoke with or were jeopardized by the wave of Palestinian violence initially centered in Jerusalem that erupted in the fall of 2015.

Throughout, the insistence of the administration and the Quartet on rhetorically encouraging and sponsoring essentially nonexistent negotiations between two genuinely distant and incompatible governments in Jerusalem and Ramallah, in the midst of a chaotic and violent Arab Middle East, inspired nothing but mistrust, and, at times, disdain on the part of both the Israeli and the Palestinian publics. Phrases like "the outlines of final status are obvious, we just need the leadership" (Secretary of State Kerry, Quartet emissary Tony Blair) and "just get to the damn table" (US Secretary of Defense Leon Panetta) generate the impression that US and other international leaders are not really familiar with the nuances of the conflict. After all, no one really knows what an agreement on refugees or the Temple Mount might conceivably look like or whether it is possible at all. And just getting to the table—as the parties did under Kerry's tutelage in 2013 and 2014, with a negative outcome a foregone conclusion and another round of Israel-Hamas fighting the ultimate result—can be genuinely counterproductive.

THE TWO SIDES' ATTITUDES AGAINST THE BACKDROP OF KERRY'S FAILURE

By 2015, a consistent majority of Israelis still supported the two-state solution. It supported US involvement in the peace process and recognized that in return for American security guarantees and backing, Israel would be expected to make territorial and other concessions. Israelis also overwhelmingly recognized their country's vital need for American support and expected their elected national leader to demonstrate a capacity to manage Jerusalem's relationship with Washington. Otherwise, as in 1992 (Yitzhak Shamir's electoral loss to Yitzhak Rabin) and 1999 (Netanyahu's defeat by Ehud Barak), they could conceivably punish that leader at the polls. Still, as we witnessed in March 2015, an Israeli leader, Netanyahu, could persuade enough of his electorate that it was sufficient to maintain close strategic coordination with only a portion of a highly divided Washington, the Republican majority in Congress, even while risking Israel's traditional ties with the US president and his administration, by bypassing the administration and addressing Congress to severely criticize the president's strategy regarding Iran-linked nuclear issues.

Yet, alongside their support for a two-state solution, most Israelis did not in 2015 believe an end to the conflict was in sight—an attitude paralleled in recent years, incidentally, by Palestinians. In the Israeli case, public lack of confidence in a peace process derived from a number of developments of recent years. One was the aggressive Arab response to unilateral Israeli redeployments from Lebanon (2000) and the Gaza Strip (2005). In the case of Gaza, settlements were removed, the 1949 green line was respected, and Palestinians were given an opportunity to engage in state-building. Yet subsequent Arab aggression appeared to signal to Israelis that no reasonable concessions on their part would satisfy Palestinians and that, indeed, ceding territory signaled weakness and invited violence that, with the outbreak of the Gaza war of 2014, involved Palestinian rocket fire directed at most population centers in Israel.

Another contributing factor was the schism between West Bank/Fatah and Gaza/Hamas, which Israelis understood to mean that Abbas could not entirely "deliver the goods" even if agreement were reached. The Islamist extremist Hamas was liable to sabotage an Israeli-Palestinian agreement through violence or, in an extreme scenario, to take over the entire newborn state through elections, as it nearly did in 2006, or by force, as it did in Gaza in 2007. Israelis understood this to be true even if, as in the spring of 2014, Fatah and Hamas registered a tenuous and superficial Palestinian unity agreement—an Israeli view borne out by the farcical nature of such repeated Palestinian unity pacts.

A third development, particularly discouraging for Israeli doves, was Abbas's rejection of Olmert's September 2008 offer—one that Israelis found singularly far-reaching, particularly with regard to an East Jerusalem Palestinian capital, Muslim state majority jurisdiction over the Temple Mount, and West Bank territorial concessions. Then there was Abbas's subsequent unwillingness less than a year later, until the eleventh hour, to challenge the hard-line Netanyahu to serious negotiations and "call his bluff," despite the latter's declared readiness to talk and partial acquiescence in a fairly prolonged settlement freeze. By 2015, it was possible to describe all three relevant local actors—Israel, the PLO/Fatah, and Hamas—as complacent, indifferent to the peace process, aggressively opposed to it, or preoccupied with other regional and domestic issues.

Taken together with the Arab revolutions surrounding Israel and the militant Islamist and Iranian intervention on the ground in Iraq and Syria that they have generated, these developments have radically reduced the size and eroded the legitimacy of the Israeli "peace camp." They seemingly refute that camp's persistent argument that an end-of-conflict agreement is achievable in short order with the right leadership. And they go a long way toward explaining the emerging dominance of the nationalistic right wing in Israeli politics.

But additional factors have also encouraged negative Israeli public attitudes toward the Obama administration. These also must be taken into account in any new attempt by Washington to foster a peace process.

One is Netanyahu's aforementioned success in nurturing alternative, nonadministration American support for his policies: from Congress, most of the American Jewish leadership, and the evangelical Christian camp. Then, too, following the emotional warmth toward Israel displayed by presidents Bill Clinton and George W. Bush (which Israelis, who crave national validation, thrive on), Obama has come off as cold and calculating—even when delivering more security backing than any of his predecessors. Not only did Obama's long-awaited visit to Israel in March 2013 fail to dispel this impression, but much of the Israeli public saw his July 2015 success in shepherding a nuclear agreement with Iran through Congress as a major instance of indifference to Israel's strategic fortunes.

Then there is the negative reaction generated in Israel (and much of the Arab world as well) by the Obama administration's policies in the region since the outbreak of so-called Arab Spring revolutions throughout the Middle East. Clearly, many of these policy decisions reflected a calculated US design to lower its Middle East profile in favor of encouraging regional coalitions and advancing domestic and East Asian trade and security priorities and could be rationalized as such in the eyes of the American public. But in Israel and among many old guard Arabs in Jordan, Egypt, Saudi Arabia, and the Persian Gulf, they merely compounded skepticism engendered by the perception of overall US weakness and American state-building failures in the Middle East.

CONCLUSION

Two important insights regarding the US role emerge from this analysis of Kerry's failed peacemaking attempt and Israeli and other attitudes toward American involvement.

First, even with active American support, yet another return to the "Oslo table" and full-fledged final-status negotiations on all outstanding issues will not succeed. Indeed, it could deepen the Israeli-Palestinian divide by adding to current frustrations. An alternative post-Oslo paradigm might be messier than Oslo and less than comprehensive, but it might also have a better chance to register desperately needed progress. That is why repeated ritual appeals by prominent international actors— mainly from the United States and the European Union—for Israel and the Palestinians to renew Oslo-based negotiations sound increasingly pathetic and, indeed, genuinely debase those pronouncing them in the eyes of anyone who is aware of how hopeless Oslo has become. They bring to mind George Orwell's dictum: "The great enemy of clear language is insincerity."

Second, in searching for this alternative paradigm, unilateral initiatives presented in recent years by the Palestinian leadership and key Israeli security figures point to the possibility of interim progress, hopefully US-sponsored (if Washington could be convinced to suffice with more modest and realistic peace objectives), that could conceivably maintain stability, move Israelis and Palestinians closer to a two-state solution, and enhance Washington's credibility as a serious peace sponsor. The next chapter looks at these ideas while acknowledging that, by and large, the Netanyahu-led rightist nationalist establishment and the Abbas-led PLO/Fatah establishment reject them.

Here we must recognize that Washington, too, does not appear to be primed to engage in serious heavy lifting in the Israeli-Palestinian sphere. If it cannot engage aggressively, based on the conviction that Israeli-Palestinian stalemate, against the backdrop of ongoing Arab revolution, seriously endangers US national security interests, then it might be well advised to stand back.

Yet, as chapter 9 discusses, ongoing stalemate between Israelis and Palestinians bespeaks scenarios that truly do threaten America's national security interests. Hence Washington has every reason to search for new solutions and paradigms, however "un-Oslo" and unorthodox they may be and however much arm-twisting they may require.

Part II

Israel Tomorrow

EIGHT

Are There Alternative Ways to Muddle Through?

If we accept the argument that the Oslo final-status paradigm had exhausted itself prior to 2013 and a new and innovative framework was required, then conceivably a more limited US initiative was called for. Without such an initiative, both Israeli-Palestinian relations and Washington's capacity to wield influence in the region might have benefited had John Kerry refrained from any involvement at all.

A careful preliminary analysis of lessons drawn from twenty years of attempts to implement the Oslo Declaration of Principles might have pointed Secretary Kerry and his team, with their admirable energies and dedication, to more modest goals. Conceivably, these could have been more feasible, given the constraints of limited presidential backing, a fading US regional profile, and recalcitrant Israeli and Palestinian partners committed to uncompromising ideological positions and preoccupied with the chaos then besetting large portions of the Middle East.

Conceivably, these ideas are still feasible, even if they remain problematic and potentially divisive. They are worthy of our attention precisely because they remain more doable than an end-of-conflict agreement while at least preventing backsliding and keeping a comprehensive solution alive. In examining them, we should keep in mind that, problematic as these options are, the two apparent alternatives are worse: doing nothing (see chapter 9) and yet again revisiting, like Kerry, the obsolete Oslo formula.

We can look for inspiration to the initiatives that have emerged independently from the two sides in recent years. These are imperfect and undoubtedly problematic, not least because they offer essentially interim rather than final steps. But they have the distinct advantage of having appeared in the field, so to speak, of enjoying at least a measure of local support on one side, and of potentially moving the conflict in the right direction toward resolution. Further, precisely because of their interim nature and their origins in the region itself, they may present less risk to an American administration or international community that adopts or supports them than embarking on another attempt to reach an end-of-conflict agreement that could instead catalyze conflict.

OPTION A: A (HOPEFULLY COORDINATED) MAJOR WEST BANK WITHDRAWAL

Ideas along this line were presented beginning in 2012 by former defense minister Shaul Mofaz; the Blue White Future movement, whose leadership features former senior security officials like Ami Ayalon, who headed the Israel navy and the Shin Bet internal security service; and the Institute for National Security Studies (INSS) under the leadership of recently retired Israel Defense Forces (IDF) Intelligence chief Amos Yadlin. In May 2015, former prime minister and defense minister Ehud Barak made a similar proposal. In July, former head of IDF Intelligence Shlomo Gazit, who was the first coordinator of Israel's operations in the West Bank and Gaza after 1967, published his own plan.

The primary rationale of these plans is their contribution to maintaining Israel as a Jewish and democratic state by reducing the scope and profile of the occupation and, correspondingly, promoting a quantitatively and qualitatively greater degree of Palestinian autonomy. In seizing the initiative, they also better position Israel for encountering the challenges posed by Arab revolution and the Iranian threat, all at a time when final-status negotiations do not appear either possible or productive.

INSS, incidentally, presents the partial withdrawal option as part of a package of ideas to be pursued simultaneously that also includes a full-fledged final-status agreement, transitional Israeli-Palestinian arrangements, and a "regional route" that is integrated with the Arab Peace Initiative (API). We will look at the latter below. The proposals for new Israeli-Palestinian agreements appear nonfeasible in view of prevailing attitudes and the leadership deficit on both sides.

The great advantage of the unilateral withdrawal approach is that, if necessary, it can be implemented without the agreement or cooperation of the Palestinian side. But by the same token, its success would be more likely with Palestinian cooperation—something only Washington may be able to deliver. The Palestine Liberation Organization (PLO) leadership has always been wary of unilateral withdrawal schemes for fear that they will leave it with considerably less than the entire territory of the West Bank but fewer means of pressuring Israel to withdraw further. This consideration led Mofaz to introduce the idea of firm international (meaning primarily American) guarantees to the effect that, following unilateral withdrawal, a final-status agreement based on the 1967 lines would be negotiated within a short period; meanwhile, Palestinian statehood would be recognized in conjunction with the first, partial withdrawal.

Another problematic aspect of the unilateral idea is possible lack of Israeli public support. This could reflect the heavy security price the Israeli public has paid for unilateral withdrawals from Lebanon in 2000 and the Gaza Strip in 2005, a trauma exploited by the political Right in arguing against any additional unilateral withdrawals. This led Yadlin to propose leaving the IDF in the Jordan Valley pending a final-status agreement, thereby giving Israel a greater measure of ongoing security control over the West Bank and applying lessons drawn from what he viewed as the mistake of withdrawing in 2005 from the Gaza-Sinai border zone, known by its IDF code name as the Philadelphi Corridor, along with the body of the Gaza Strip. Barak concurs, arguing somewhat speciously that in the Jordan Valley—which was empty except for the town of Jericho and nomadic Bedouin when Israel began settling it shortly after 1967— "we have had a Jewish majority for generations." Gazit would leave most of the IDF presence in place pending Palestinian readiness to take security responsibility and negotiate permanent borders and a refugee solution. Yet any ongoing Israeli military presence in the territories would undoubtedly render the Israeli withdrawal less attractive to the Palestinians.

How much territory would Israel relinquish unilaterally in the West Bank, and would it remove settlements? The proposals vary. Some seek withdrawal to the security fence line, leaving Israel in full control of only about 9 percent of the territory, including East Jerusalem and all of the settlement blocs, with financial incentives to leave offered to settlers beyond the fence. Others suggest a more modest move, withdrawing from only 10 or 20 percent of the West Bank and little, if any, settlement removal. Blue White Future would leave Israeli security forces in place in Areas B and C (the latter comprising nearly 60 percent) of the West Bank pending a peace agreement, while declaring a future border along the security fence line and providing incentives for settlers in Area C beyond the fence to leave. Gazit suggests a total settlement construction freeze, declaration of end of occupation throughout the West Bank, and legislation of a compensation mechanism for settlers who agree to voluntary evacuation, but no compulsory evacuation and no final IDF withdrawal pending a negotiated final-status agreement.

Obviously, the more territory turned over to Palestinian rule, the more settlements removed or at least incentives offered for settlers to leave, and the less residual Israeli security presence, the more likely the withdrawal is to attain the presumed objective of such an interim move: expanding Palestinian autonomy, discouraging violence bred by Palestinian frustration, nourishing and sustaining the two-state process and its Palestinian and Israeli supporters, and encouraging the sides to follow up with serious final-status negotiations. US support, along with commitments to the Palestinians regarding the final-status sovereign and territorial outcome and to Israel regarding the security risks it undertakes, would be vital to both sides—even if the PLO officially rejects the initiative. However, if West Bank territory whose control is relinquished by Israel falls into the hands of Hamas or some other extremist group, the result of withdrawal could eventually be more violence against Israel, following the pattern established by the Gaza withdrawal.

OPTION B: A JORDANIAN ROLE FOR THE HOLY PLACES

Yet another outside-the-box alternative might seek to isolate the pre-1967 narrative-based issue of holy places and—assuming that the parties insist on discussing it forthwith—to render it more manageable by inviting Jordan to convene and manage a separate negotiating track dedicated to it alone. The Jordan-Israel peace treaty of 1994 and a 2013 Jordan-PLO agreement recognize Jordan's preeminent role on the Arab side regarding Jerusalem holy sites.

Progress toward an agreed compromise status for the holy places, spearheaded by an agreed third party with an internationally recognized role, could conceivably catalyze progress elsewhere in the Israeli-Palestinian equation. At a minimum, even without touching on the core narrative issue of the significance of the Temple Mount for Jews, it could radically reduce the violence and confrontation that in 2014 and 2015 were becoming endemic there and at additional disputed holy places. Only a mutually recognized third-party authority could conceivably begin to clarify the real nature of an agreed "status quo" on the Mount (who can visit, who can pray, when, and where)—the issue that sparked the extreme outburst of violence of October 2015. Jordan, however, might not be willing to undertake this task, and both Israel and the PLO might be reluctant to enable a Jordanian role.

OPTION C: THE INTERNATIONAL
COMMUNITY TAKING CHARGE

The Palestinian leadership wants the United Nations to intervene; the Israeli leadership does not. The Palestinian position derives from weakness; its point of departure is that Israel "has the upper hand" (a phrase used repeatedly in negotiations by Yasser Arafat) in the relationship, and accordingly it welcomes any and all third-party reinforcements. Israel, correspondingly, assesses that "internationalization" of the conflict will stack the odds against it and expose it to diplomatic and perhaps economic pressures that disregard its security vulnerabilities and core values. A long succession of Israeli governments can cite endless examples of the application of double standards by international organizations, from the United Nations through UNESCO to the International Criminal Court, to back up the case against international involvement.

Yet, if nothing else works and stalemate is driving Israelis and Palestinians toward a hellish one-state situation, even resorting to the UN Security Council might be the lesser evil, particularly if a still-friendly United States can insist on relative balance in whatever resolution emerges with the objective of advancing a solution. By late 2014, a growing number of Israeli peace activists like Shaul Arieli of the security-dove Council for Peace and Security and researchers like Oded Eran of INSS were coming around to embracing or endorsing the idea of a balanced Security Council resolution. Some of the schemes broached by Israelis overambitiously called for parallel limited initiatives by Israel, the PLO, and even Gaza-based Hamas, but the core innovation was a readiness to countenance UN intervention of some sort.

By 2015, the United Nations constituted the Palestinian default option. Encouragingly, however, what the PLO and others were asking of the United Nations appeared to be relatively far from the kind of comprehensive diktat that is anathema to Israelis.

Mahmoud Abbas's experience in direct negotiations with Ehud Olmert in 2008—following on the first final-status negotiating failure in 2000 at Camp David between Ehud Barak and Yasser Arafat—must be viewed as a critical juncture in the current Palestinian leader's understanding of his own capacity to end the conflict. Abbas had rejected the farthest-reaching Israeli peace proposal yet because it still did not come close to accommodating the core demands of his constituents, most of whom are diaspora-based refugees, particularly regarding the pre-1967 narrative-based issues of holy places and the right of return.

As noted earlier, this suggests that the Oslo formula of linking all final-status issues in an agreement will continue to founder on these two issues. Both the 2000 and the 2008 negotiations demonstrated that the post-1967 disputes—over territory, statehood, and security—are relatively more amenable to agreement. In contrast, the differences grounded in both sides' deeper, pre-1967 historical narratives are an important reason for nearly twenty years of failed efforts.

We have already explored in historical depth the perception that the Palestinian demand that Israel recognize the right of return for Palestinian refugees implies a tacit acknowledgment by the state of Israel that it was born in sin in 1948. Similarly, Israel perceives the Palestinian assertion that there never was a temple on the Temple Mount and that Israel has no inherent rights there as a denial of its national and historical roots. These Palestinian positions in turn explain Israel's counterdemand of recent years—itself undoubtedly also a narrative deal breaker because it is blatantly unacceptable to the Arab camp—that the Palestinians recognize Israel not merely as a sovereign state but as a Jewish state on the soil of Palestine.

The United Nations created Israel as a Jewish state, and Israel's Declaration of Independence reiterates this determination. Hence, on the one hand, Israel's demand for yet another round of Jewish state recognition, this time from its neighbors, can be deemed unnecessary and provocative. Yet, on the other, Arab rejection of the Jewish state designation clearly reflects a bias whereby Jews are defined not as an indigenous Middle East people with the right to self-determination but as members of a Western religion that stole land belonging to the Muslim heritage. This prejudicial approach probably cannot be expunged, but it can be radically marginalized by the signing of a two-state agreement.

Abbas, then, has turned to the United Nations not only because the Palestinian state-building enterprise in the West Bank has proven unsuccessful but, conceivably, also because it is clear that Oslo-based final-status negotiations, even if they reconvene, cannot succeed in ending all claims. In this sense, Abbas's intransigence regarding the contents of a full final-status package, no less than Benjamin Netanyahu's, has brought Abbas to the United Nations since 2011.

At the United Nations—unlike in bilateral negotiations—Abbas appears to be prepared to accept international determination of the 1967 borders and a Palestinian capital in East Jerusalem as the defining parameters of a Palestinian state, with the narrative-based issues of refugees and holy places delinked from this package and left to further negotiations. Even if Israel and Palestine subsequently fail to agree on these pre-1967 narrative issues—as well they might—we still emerge from the United Nations with the determination of a two-state reality and with a conflict whose manageability is no longer held hostage to insurmountable existential questions.

True, Abbas has consistently shrouded his UN initiative in a cloud of alternative policy departures such as dismantling the Palestinian Authority, resigning, reconciling with Hamas and holding new elections, and pursuing Israel in a variety of international tribunals. And he still feels politically obliged to publicly profess adherence to the full Oslo menu. Besides, by late 2015 his grasp on power, even in the West Bank alone, appeared to be so tentative as to raise doubts about the efficacy of any initiative associated with him. But here we should look at what he does, not what he says: the real significance of his repeated UN initiatives could be to turn the conflict into a more manageable and limited state-to-state negotiation.

Yet a wary Israel would need guarantees as to where this was heading. If Washington was willing (the Europeans and Russians are already predisposed in this direction), the request for UN recognition of a Palestinian state could conceivably be leveraged into a new two-state paradigm—an updated UN Security Council Resolution 242 that in effect replaces the Oslo Accords—that serves Israel's vital needs as well as those of the Palestinians. This would require a radical change in existing US policy regarding a UN or alternative international role, as well as a willingness to incur some opposition on the part of both parties to the conflict. On the other hand, it would build on President Barack Obama's May 2011 proposal that the issues of territories and security be awarded priority in negotiations.

A win-win UN resolution regarding Palestinian statehood—or a formula nurtured in an alternative forum like the Quartet (the United States, European Union, United Nations, and Russia)—could, for example, go a long way toward satisfying key demands of both sides and the United States by undertaking to do the following:

1. Balance the declarative creation of a Palestinian state by recalling that the United Nations created Israel as a Jewish state (thereby obviating the need for explicit Palestinian recognition of a Jewish state). The resolution would call on both states to provide equal rights to minorities.

2. Balance recognition of the 1967 lines as the basis for a shared border by recognizing the need for agreed territorial swaps—something the PLO has in any event accepted and Netanyahu reportedly agreed to in principle in 2013 and 2014.

3. Balance recognition of a Palestinian capital in East Jerusalem with long-delayed international recognition of Israel's capital in West Jerusalem.

4. Recognize that extending the authority and status of a sovereign Palestinian state to the Gaza Strip will depend on effective control there by the legitimate and internationally recognized Palestinian government. Otherwise, if and when Israel retaliates against attack from Gaza, it will be attacking sovereign Palestine and jeopardizing the entire two-state structure.

5. Relegate all relevant issues involved in implementing this resolution to direct, bilateral negotiations, beginning with the post-1967 issues of borders, a Palestinian capital, settlements, water, and security where progress has been registered in earlier talks.

6. Recognize that negotiations regarding the right of return of 1948 refugees and holy places—both intractable pre-1967 narrative issues that have thwarted negotiations for years—must be held between the two parties only after they are functioning state neighbors with a stake in coexistence and the capacity to maintain the peace even in the absence of agreement on these issues.

7. Recognize Israel's legitimate security needs as it concedes West Bank territory through negotiations and offer UN (and separately

US) guarantees for them, including a nonmilitarized Palestinian state.

8. Call upon the Arab states to begin seriously implementing the concessions they offer under the Arab Peace Initiative as an additional incentive to Israel at a time when both Israel and the functioning Arab states face common enemies.

Such an approach to leveraging the Palestinian UN initiative would not end the conflict or end all claims. A lot of negotiating in accordance with that initiative—about border delineation, the shape of the Palestinian capital, timetables, security, and so forth—would still be called for. Separately, it might still take a generation or more to resolve the now delinked pre-1967 narrative issues. Moreover, if the entire purpose of a UN Security Council resolution becomes merely to oblige Israelis and Palestinians to sit down again and negotiate, without also presenting a new negotiating paradigm that bypasses the obstacles posed by Oslo, then it is likely to prove as counterproductive as the 2013–2014 Kerry initiative.

Regarding the delinking of pre-1967 narrative issues, overcoming both Israeli and Palestinian opposition would require a strong US stand. Washington would have to remind the Israeli public that ending the occupation and maintaining Israel as a secure Jewish and democratic state constitute a far greater reward than holding out for unattainable concessions on intractable narrative issues. It could suggest to the Palestinians that a sovereign state is an attainable goal that overrides their fixation with the unattainable right of return. This win-win approach, whose terms correspond fully with existing US commitments to Israel, like those set out in George W. Bush's 2004 letter to Ariel Sharon, could render the conflict far more manageable. From there on, settling the outstanding disagreements would be a state-to-state affair rather than a negotiation between Israel and a national liberation movement whose main constituency lies outside the territory under discussion.

Make no mistake: The only power conceivably capable of marshaling the international community to move in this direction while reassuring the Israeli public regarding its core interests is the United States. Even if France acts on its policy pronouncements of early 2015 and introduces a two-state resolution to the Security Council, the Europeans as a whole are unable and unwilling to act strongly and in concert. And Russia and China lack the motivation and the influence over Israel. I can testify that my personal efforts to cultivate interest in a "new 242" option between 2011 and 2015 produced no more than polite interest (and deference to Washington) in London, Paris, Berlin, Oslo, and Moscow and studied disinterest in the US capital.

At the time of this writing, Washington's pique with the Netanyahu government over the Iran issue could suggest a UN route on the Palestinian issue as a vehicle for reasserting US leadership concerning Israel-related issues in the face of a hostile Israeli government. Yet Washington was either not interested or holding out Security Council recognition of a Palestinian state as a stick to persuade Prime Minister Netanyahu to maintain his pro forma and meaningless adherence to a two-state solution. Then, too, the 2016 US presidential elections could turn this issue into a political football and dissuade the administration from adopting such a potentially controversial approach.

OPTION D: THE ARAB PEACE INITIATIVE

A number of prominent Israeli centrists are convinced that Israel has merely to declare acceptance of the Arab Peace Initiative (for earlier references to the API, see chapters 6 and 7) in order to launch a process whereby the moderate pro-Western Arab states, led by Egypt, Jordan, Saudi Arabia, and the United Arab Emirates, enter the fray and provide the moderation lacking in the PLO and the security reassurances that Israel needs to bring about a two-state solution. Some right-wing Israelis, like Avigdor Lieberman, who served as foreign minister until 2015, profess also to believe that this same Arab coalition will somehow bail Israel out by offering a regional strategic framework for an Israeli-Palestinian deal that partially absolves Israel of the need to make painful territorial and other compromises to the Palestinians.

The point of departure for these initiatives is the encouragement and occasional security facilitation provided to Israel in recent years by Egypt, Jordan, and Saudi Arabia against the backdrop of shared tension or conflict with militant Islam in the form of Gaza-based Hamas, al-Qaeda, and the Islamic State and shared suspicion of Iran and its motives. Yet these same pro-Western Sunni Arab countries resolutely refuse to venture beyond clandestine strategic cooperation and proceed to normalization of ties with Israel unless and until Israel registers significant progress toward resolving the Palestinian issue. The so-called street, meaning public opinion, in these countries would probably never countenance anything less. Israeli and well-meaning Western leaders who advocate this API-related course of action appear to be woefully ignorant of core Arab attitudes toward Jews and Israel.

There are additional obstacles to embracing the API. In 2015 the Arab world was in such a state of disarray, anarchy, and violence that it was not easily described as a coherent peacemaker. Then, too, the pro-API camp tends to ignore or belittle the "landmines" embedded in the API: the explicit refusal by the Arab states to absorb 1948 refugees themselves; the mention of UN General Assembly Resolution 194, which calls for the original refugees' return to their homes where practical but is understood by Arabs as ratifying the right of return of successive generations of refugees; and the apparent ongoing insistence that Israel make peace with Syria even in its current state of anarchy and fragmentation in order to qualify for normalization of relations with the Arab world.

Still, Israel has relatively little to lose by publicly accepting the API, even with reservations, and offering to discuss implementation with the Arab League. At a minimum, conditional acceptance of the API could gain Israel time to maneuver in its interaction with the region and the Palestinians. This would also appear to be a fundamental condition for encouraging the highly unlikely but not entirely unrealistic contingency whereby one or more Sunni Arab states, under the extreme duress of militant Islamist or Iranian-backed Shiite aggression, undertake to bring their relationship with Israel into the open as a means of improving their defensive capabilities (see chapter 10).

OPTION E: A STABLE, LONG-TERM CEASE-FIRE WITH HAMAS IN GAZA

The Hamas leadership in Gaza refuses to negotiate directly with any Israeli leadership. Hamas, the Palestinian branch of the Muslim Brotherhood, rejects Israel's existence and continues to embrace the notorious anti-Semitic forgery *The Protocols of the Elders of Zion* as a foundation stone of its belief system. But after three highly destructive wars with Israel in less than a decade, the political leadership of Hamas appeared interested in the spring and summer of 2015 in exploring proposals tendered by Turkish, Qatari, and European mediators for a long-term cease-fire with Israel. According to most media reports, the proposal would entail a three- to five- or even eight-year agreement, opening of Gaza's border with Israel to extensive commerce, and possibly even discussion of constructing air- and seaports for the strip, with agreed security precautions.

This was not the first time the idea of a separate cease-fire between Israel and Gaza-based Hamas had surfaced. In the present case, it appeared to be a spin-off of developments in the approach to the region of Qatar and Saudi Arabia as both sought more proactive roles in the Sunni-Shiite wars in the Levant and as Riyadh became deeply involved in the Yemeni civil war. Specifically, a Hamas-Israel deal brokered by one or both of these Sunni Gulf powers would strike a blow against Shiite Iran's influence with the Sunni Hamas. Nor did either Gulf state seem particularly sensitive to protests from the West Bank–based PLO, Israel's official Palestinian negotiating partner, insofar as all attempts to date to broker reunification between the PLO and Hamas, and correspondingly between the West Bank and Gaza Strip, have failed due to a combination of Palestinian weakness and the two movements' religious-ideological incompatibility.

From Israel's standpoint, a right-wing Israeli government might conceivably be more inclined than a left-center government to explore a possible deal with Gaza-based Hamas. This would presumably provide a much needed respite from violence on the Gaza front while not tying the government's hands in the West Bank, where it would seek to proceed with settlement expansion and a territorial grab, and not obliging it to negotiate seriously with the PLO, which would correspondingly perceive itself as having been isolated by a Gaza cease-fire. To the extent such a measure more or less permanently fragments the Palestinian polity, this is not necessarily objectionable to the Israeli Right, which in any case is not a willing candidate for a genuine two-state agreement with a unified Palestinian state.

On the other hand, a deal with Hamas, while merely a cease-fire, nevertheless risks being perceived as violating explicit understandings between Israel and the Quartet (the United States, United Nations, European Union, and Russia) concerning conditions Hamas must satisfy to qualify as a peace partner: recognizing Israel, ceasing terrorism, and accepting the Oslo Accords. Accordingly, an Israel-Hamas long-term cease-fire, even if clothed as a "humanitarian" rather than political measure, could conceivably disrupt Israel's relations with important international actors.

Here it bears emphasizing that, alongside the obvious advantages of nonbelligerency between Israel and Hamas, a Gaza cease-fire would in no way be based on mutual trust between the two sides. Indeed, from Israel's standpoint, it might well prove to be a temporary arrangement during which the forces of militant Islam would seek to arm and fortify the strip for an eventual return to belligerency against Israel. Moreover, an Israel-Gaza cease-fire does not end Israel's conflict with either Palestinian entity, does not even begin to satisfy Arab and international requirements for a Palestinian solution, and does not alleviate the demographic threat to Israel's long-term status as a democratic, Jewish state. Further, it would likely alienate not only the PLO in the West Bank but also anti-Islamist Egypt—a key security partner for Israel in dealing with the regional Islamist threat based in Sinai and elsewhere. Notably, the powerful Hamas military wing reportedly opposed the spring–summer 2015 long-term cease-fire initiative, thereby posing yet another formidable obstacle even to preliminary agreement.

CONCLUSION

None of these or similar proposals for limited progress seem very likely to be broached, much less implemented, by any of the major involved parties in the second decade of the twenty-first century. Israeli governments with their heavy settler, right-wing, and religious-messianist component will not be interested. Washington remains committed to the failed Oslo approach or prefers studied inaction. The PLO does advance the idea of a UN statehood resolution, but along terms unacceptable even to a moderate Israeli government and on behalf of a Palestinian leadership bereft of genuine governmental and territorial authority. If the UN Security Council does pass a resolution, the government of Israel will almost certainly opt to ignore it or negotiate it to death. The Arab world is busy with its own mess.

Yet ideas for limited progress that do not require immediate Israeli-Palestinian negotiations are worth discussing. These are probably the only options for muddling through or managing the conflict that are both reasonable and feasible for the years to come. On balance, even in a worst-case situation following some sort of West Bank withdrawal, unilateral or partial, Israel is arguably better off rebuffing rocket and tunnel attackers from there on behalf of an overwhelming consensus of Israelis than trying to absorb that territory's Arab residents and thereby gradually becoming an ugly, internally conflicted, and externally provocative Jewish-Arab binational entity—the topic of the next chapter.

NINE

On the Slippery Slope toward a Binational Israel

In recent years, Israel has been the target of growing international criticism and an international delegitimization movement. Ostensibly this can largely be attributed to Israeli settlement and occupation policies, the absence of an Israeli-Palestinian peace process, antidemocratic domestic moves in Israel directed against minorities and human rights advocates, and Palestinian preference for delegitimization campaigns over new attempts at negotiation.

Some of the international criticism, where not engaged in delegitimizing Israel's very existence, is undoubtedly justified. But some appears to rest on a poor understanding of regional circumstances and their understandable effect on Israel's national psyche. Among those circumstances are the rise of militant Islam around nearly all of Israel's borders, severe disunity within the Palestinian national movement, ongoing Palestinian terrorism and rocket attack campaigns from Gaza, and the conditions that led to the failure of recent attempts to foster a peace process between Palestinians and Israelis (see chapter 7).

But if a degree of controversy surrounds the legitimacy of official Israeli policies regarding the Palestinian issue, there can be little doubt that the Israeli political majority has turned to the right. At the extreme edge of this development—an increasingly thick edge where around one-third of members of the Knesset can be found—the Israeli political scene features a growing number of factions and persons who identify with antidemocratic measures domestically and voice outspoken opposition to the two-state solution.

Note that the growth of this opposition is paralleled on the Palestinian side, where polls show the pro-two-state-solution majority constantly shrinking as more and more Palestinians reconcile themselves to what they see as a South African–style dynamic in which eventually, by dint of Arab population growth and international pressure, one-state Israel becomes binational or even Arab ruled. Note also that, as mentioned in chapter 4, the elite leadership of the Arab citizens of Israel has for nearly a decade actively advocated a binational one-state solution based on a denial of Jewish national rights—a movement to delegitimize Israel from within that provides political ammunition to Israel's extreme Right.

Is this a slippery slope leading Israel toward some version of apartheid, ostensibly as a framework for managing rather than resolving the Palestinian issue? Prime Minister Benjamin Netanyahu and his associates regularly speak of "managing" the conflict as their default option. A growing and increasingly influential faction of right-wing Israelis is openly advocating ideas for annexing all or most of the West Bank and relegating West Bank Palestinians to a more or less permanent status approaching apartheid. Members of this faction registered spectacular gains in Israel's 2013 Knesset elections and captured positions of influence in the coalition subsequently formed by Netanyahu. Interestingly, in the March 2015 Knesset elections they did not augment their influence, but only because their parties yielded votes to the ruling Likud thanks to Netanyahu's last-minute scare tactics focusing on the threat posed by a united Israeli Arab party and by the Israeli Arab vote—hardly a development that Israeli liberals can take comfort in.

The atomization of Israeli politics is not over, with parties increasingly fielding five to fifteen Knesset members and coalitions demonstrating instability and generating absurd and extreme legislative initiatives serving narrow political purposes. The Israeli political scene thus remains highly conducive to manipulation by the most determined and dynamic of the factions: the ultranationalist, pro-settler, and settler right wing.

THE CURRENT SITUATION IS NOT APARTHEID

The situation in Israel and Palestine in late 2015 cannot be described as apartheid. Each sector of Arabs living under partial or complete Israeli control offers a different, highly nuanced picture of discrimination for which Israel is not entirely to blame but is inevitably held to account by the Arab world and the international community. To substantiate this argument, let us look briefly at each of these sectors.

If West Bank Palestinians suffer today from restricted political rights, they and the Arab world are as much to blame as Israel. Their leadership rejected Israeli peace offers in 2000 and 2008 that would have radically enhanced their sovereign status. Their education system and public diplomacy continue to delegitimize Israel. Yet because the Palestinians are stateless underdogs, and because they have successfully cultivated their refugee and "victim" status in international eyes for nearly seventy years,

Israel takes far more blame than they for the conflict. Moreover, the ongoing spread of Israeli settlements in Judea and Samaria appears to belie Israeli protestations of good intentions regarding the emergence of a viable Palestinian state in the West Bank.

But at least in the West Bank the Palestinians enjoy considerable autonomy and a thriving business and educational sector, along with a leadership that subscribes publicly to nonviolence and claims to adhere to the two-state idea (even as it proffers peace conditions, particularly on the pre-1967 narrative issues, that rule out any reasonable resolution of the conflict). In contrast, the Gaza Strip under Hamas rule rejects a peace process. Israel withdrew its settlers and soldiers in 2005 and, together with the international community, offered a menu of state-building arrangements that Palestinians quickly scuttled. This led to a spiral of Israeli economic restrictions and repeated Gazan attacks against Israeli civilians that developed into mini-wars in 2008 and 2009, 2012, and 2014, in which rockets fired from Gaza targeted larger and larger portions of Israel and the Israel Defense Forces (IDF) responded harshly.

In any case, Israelis who advocate discriminatory solutions for the Palestinians of the West Bank totally ignore the Gaza Strip in their calculations and projections. Note that Gaza, unlike the West Bank, enjoys a common border with the Arab world (Egypt); under different Palestinian leadership capable of working with the anti-Islamist Egyptians, Gaza could function as a fully independent entity.

The three hundred thousand or so Arab denizens of East Jerusalem, who have Israeli residency rights, can achieve Israeli citizenship only if they apply for it. For the most part they do not, whether due to pressure from their Arab neighbors or for patriotic Palestinian motives. Nor do they exercise their right to vote in Jerusalem municipal elections, thereby foregoing the opportunity, given that they constitute nearly 40 percent of the city's population, to exercise serious influence over municipal affairs and to mitigate the socioeconomic conditions that by all accounts currently render them second-class residents.

As noted in chapter 4, the 1.3 million Palestinian Arab citizens of Israel claim discrimination and make demands regarding the nature of the Israeli state. These claims and demands warrant serious attention. But these Israelis have full voting rights and—in recognition of their kinship with an Arab world still in conflict with Israel—fewer obligations, such as military service, than most Israelis. In many areas of Israeli commercial and professional life, they have in recent years registered impressive steps toward integration. While their political leadership aggressively pursues a call for Israel to become a "state of all its citizens," rather than the state of the Jewish people, and while, after all, the Arab citizens of Israel voted for these leaders, polls indicate that for a large proportion of them, demands for equal communal rights and social and economic opportunities, even in a Jewish state, consistently suffice.

Still, the provocative demands of the Israeli Arab political leadership, coupled with an ugly ultranationalist trend among Israeli rightists, have repeatedly generated legislative initiatives in the Knesset that elevate Jewish components of the Israeli state character and relegate Arab citizens to second-class status. By late 2015, nearly all of these initiatives—for example, to cancel Arabic as a national language with equal status to Hebrew, require loyalty oaths, and give the state's Jewish character preference over its democratic aspect in defining Israel constitutionally—had failed to win Knesset approval. But they were steadily gaining ground at the political-electoral level.

The growing camp of Israelis who seek to freeze or adjust the status of West Bank Palestinians at a level lower than sovereignty are described here as tilting toward apartheid not because they specifically advocate a pre-1994 South African model or because they acknowledge that what they advocate is apartheid. They do not, at least not openly and probably not consciously. Rather, the apartheid argument is offered here because this camp of Israelis seeks to permanently deprive the West Bank Palestinian population of most of the land that, with massive international support, it claims, to render it incapable of self-determination and sovereignty, and to deprive it permanently of comprehensive human and sovereign rights. If the Palestinian citizenship of West Bank Arabs is limited exclusively to West Bank Bantustans, presumably corresponding with Areas A and B, and these are systematically and structurally deprived of key human and citizenship rights and are economically dependent on Israel, this will be apartheid. This is the same camp that seeks to demote Israel's Arab Palestinian citizens to second-class status and leave the Jerusalem Arab population in less-than-equal status. Indeed, the movement restrictions imposed by the Netanyahu government on the Palestinian residents of outlying village neighborhoods of East Jerusalem, like Jebel Mukaber, during the unrest of October 2015 were dangerously reminiscent of classic South African apartheid pass laws.

Taken together (without the Gaza Strip!) these Palestinians number over 4 million. If and as they are forced to accept permanent second-class status within Israel or under Israeli rule by over 6 million Israeli Jews who increasingly answer to a right-wing pro-settler leadership, a new demographic-political reality will emerge in which Israel is either a binational Jewish-Arab state or openly apartheid in nature.

Here a word is in order regarding demographic statistics. Some Israeli right-wingers argue persistently that Palestinian population statistics are exaggerated. They insist on reducing figures for the West Bank Palestinian population by 1 million. Most reputable demographers cast heavy doubt on this contention, which appears politically motivated. The Palestinian statistics bureau estimates that Arabs (including in the Gaza Strip) will outnumber Jews in the Holy Land by 7.2 million to 6.9 million by the end of the decade. The bureau said on January 1, 2015, that 6.08 million

Arabs live in Israel, the West Bank, Gaza, and East Jerusalem, alongside 6.1 million Israeli Jews (while 7.5 million Palestinians live in the diaspora). Official Israeli statistics are roughly comparable. But even assuming the right-wing doubters are correct and there are only 3.5 million Palestinians in the West Bank, East Jerusalem, and Israel proper, they still constitute about one-third the population of an Israel that absorbs the West Bank, thus still rendering Israel a binational entity that will be hard put to remain democratic yet claim the demographic or constitutional status of a Jewish state.

My objective here is, first, to take a brief look at the surprisingly diverse views of a number of leading Jewish advocates of what appear to be apartheid-like concepts in Israel. Then, based on the most workable synthesis of these views, I shall attempt to describe what Israel will look like and how it will function—or, far more likely, malfunction spectacularly—domestically, regionally, and internationally, if these advocates have their way.

CHARACTERISTICS OF THE PROTOAPARTHEID RIGHT WING'S OVERALL APPROACH

In analyzing the views of the pro-settler right-wing ideological vanguard regarding the fate of the West Bank and its Arab population, a number of characteristics stand out. For one, in some cases the right wing's ideas derive from a genuine sense that the settlements and the occupation, while fully justified ideologically, have placed Palestinians in an unfair and untenable situation and are increasingly compromising Israel's international standing. Hence the need to adjust the status of West Bank Arabs in a manner that, under this concept, renders it more just, but without granting Palestinian statehood.

Many advocates of apartheid-like solutions appear to have, or at least profess, no fear of international sanctions: the world, they believe—citing precedents in Israel's short history—will acquiesce in Israel's claim to exclusive or near-total sovereignty west of the Jordan River if Israelis are united and determined in establishing facts on the ground. Increasingly, they feel they can rely on US support or at least neutrality: a late 2014 poll found that fully 34 percent of Americans actually support a one-state solution.

Here's how one blogger with close links to the Diaspora, David M. Weinberg, comprehensively defined these positions in the *Jerusalem Post* in December 2014:

> Israel and the Jewish world frets [*sic*] far too much about vacuous resolutions that ceremoniously pronounce upon Palestinian political rights. . . . What counts is aliyah [Jewish immigration to Israel], the Israeli birth rate, building starts in Jerusalem, the strength of our mili-

tary, the tone and tenor of our educational, cultural and legal institutions, the Jewish and democratic fabric of our society, the depth of our belief and loyalty to Jewish and Zionist principles. That's what really counts.

Everything else—our foreign and diplomatic relations, and our standing in the international community—will fall into place if we Israelis are united and confident in our creed.

This approach willfully rejects the question of whether United Nations recognition of Palestinian observer-state status, growing recognition of a virtual Palestinian "state" by European countries, or even full-fledged UN recognition of statehood renders annexing all or part of the West Bank increasingly problematic in terms of international reaction. In all demographic and political calculations, it ignores not only the future status of the Gaza Strip but also the three-hundred-thousand-strong Palestinian population of East Jerusalem, which Israel has annexed. Indeed, some members of this pro-settler vanguard insist, with no recognizable basis in reality, that there are 1 million fewer Arabs in the West Bank than everyone thinks, and that 1 million Jews will soon immigrate to Israel from the West (and that no Israelis will join the hundreds of thousands who have already opted to emigrate), thereby "righting" the demographic balance for the foreseeable future.

Politically, this camp insists it can ignore the dwindling majority of Israelis, including some on the political Right, who still favor eventual partition and a two-state solution with a viable Palestinian partner. It does so because it doesn't believe that Israel has a viable partner for an agreement. While many Israelis share skepticism regarding a partner, the quasi-apartheid advocates go much further by insisting that because the Palestinians will never really abandon the right of return of more than 5 million descendants of the 1948 refugees, and because their ultimate goal will remain elimination of the state of Israel, no accommodation is possible. Thus some of these advocates conveniently reject the notion of interim solutions under which Israel surrenders West Bank territory in order to keep the two-state solution alive precisely by insisting that any agreement must include Palestinian acceptance of an end of conflict that resolves issues like refugee right of return.

Many Israelis have doubts regarding Palestinian motives. But many also believe they need a two-state solution and must come up with concessions to generate it in order to "save Israel from itself" in terms of the evils of occupation, to preserve Israel's place in the world community, and to ensure its survival as a Jewish and democratic state. The ideological settler vanguard generally rejects these motives, with the singular exception of the need to maintain a Jewish state.

Indeed, most of these advocates will have no part of any peace process. They, along with many on the more moderate right wing, blame not themselves but the Oslo process of the past twenty years, with its withdrawals and settlement dismantling, for Israel's isolation, for terrorism, and for the schisms in Israeli society. "It's [the Zionist Left's] talk of separation, that [patronizing attitude], that generates the hatred that prevents us from arriving at a logical solution," states Reuven Rivlin, a leading one-state advocate who is now president of Israel. Others, ignoring the occupation and the first intifada, claim that until twenty years ago the settlers and West Bank Palestinians shared all roads and services and coexisted in an idyllic atmosphere.

Some nobly profess to reject the notion of ethnic divisions between Jews and Arabs. Yet those who advocate annexing all the territories into a single state insist that, somehow, the post-annexation Israel most of them envisage will remain Jewish and Zionist in its spirit and symbols while awarding Palestinian Arabs "full personal or civil rights" but not, by omission, national rights. In other words, the state will be more Jewish than democratic. Hence they reject leftist post-Zionist and Israeli Arab advocacy that Israel become truly binational or a state of all its citizens.

Here some right-wing advocates fall back on nineteenth-century European liberal ideas of national and cultural autonomy embodied in early Revisionist Zionist movement thinking. They also almost inevitably allow that rights will be awarded to annexed Palestinians only "eventually," "gradually," and "according to circumstances," thereby perhaps deliberately blurring the ideological and demographic borders between a binational solution and an apartheid state. In anticipation of intervention by Israel's liberal-leaning High Court of Justice—until now a frequent defender of human and civil rights in Israel and among Palestinians under Israeli occupation—the pro-settler right wing constantly seeks to legislate sharp limits on the High Court's constitutional authority to repeal or even question ultranationalistic and antidemocratic legislation. Further, a growing segment of the messianist right wing is also constantly pushing the envelope regarding the need to enable Jewish prayer on the Temple Mount or even to rebuild the Temple—a highly incendiary issue for Muslims everywhere.

WHAT THEY SAY

The best way of comprehending this approach is to listen to its proponents. Here is a sampling of the variety of solutions the new ideological vanguard of the mainstream pro-settler Right is offering up to the Israeli public.

The High-Tech Politician

Naftali Bennett, the dynamic leader of the HaBait HaYehudi (Jewish Home) party which garnered twelve Knesset seats in the 2013 elections before dropping in 2015 to eight (mandates that moved to the Likud and thereby stayed within the right-wing majority), proposes that Israel annex the 60 percent of the West Bank encompassed in Area C and still under full Israeli occupation and award the three hundred thousand Palestinians living there Israeli citizenship (three hundred thousand is the UN figure; some settlers interested in annexing Area C claim it holds only around sixty thousand Arabs). The remaining 40 percent of the territory comprising Areas A and B, with their large Palestinian population, will have "full autonomy with transportation continuity. . . . We'll improve the lives of the Arabs and dispense with superfluous international and humanitarian pressure."

Bennett understands this is not a full-fledged solution but argues that Israel's "Arab problem . . . has no solution." If the West Bank Palestinians do not like the autonomy imposed upon them, Israel will have to respond brutally to "violations of the ceasefire." We have to recognize we live in a dangerous neighborhood, he and his supporters state, and that this is the best we can do. He does not seem to be aware that his approach might be understood as paternalistic or colonialist. Rather, it is the least of all evils.

Bennett also appears to believe, like many on the pro-settlement Right, that time is on Israel's side. In a June 2015 speech, after acknowledging that regarding Judea and Samaria he would "agree not to agree" with those who oppose his views, he proceeded to argue that at least Israel's 1981 annexation of the Golan Heights, on its border with Syria and currently vital to Israel's security in confronting the chaos in that country, can no longer be an issue of contention with the world. The implication was clear: given time, the world will also accept the rationale for Bennett's scheme for the West Bank.

Former Council of West Bank–Gaza Settlers (Yesha Council) chair Adi Mintz actually preceded Bennett with the proposal to annex 60 percent of the West Bank. But unlike Bennett, Mintz does have a solution for the other 40 percent, suggesting "a comprehensive regional political solution, in the more distant future." This roughly corresponds with right-wing suggestions to solve the Palestinian issue within the framework of the Arab Peace Initiative, under an interpretation that somehow expects the Arab states to compensate West Bank Palestinians for ending up in an enclave surrounded by Israeli territory. And until then? Assuming Mintz has something specific in mind behind this deliberately fuzzy formula, it is probably a euphemism for what one of his successors, Danny Dayan, proposes.

The Settler Mathematician

Danny Dayan, a recent chairman of the Yesha Council, is, like Bennett, a veteran of the high-tech sector (Dayan was trained as a mathematician) who seems to favor engineering solutions for complex political problems.

He opposes annexation since it will invite international condemnation and pressure. Instead, Israel needs to "change the variables" so as to "improve the formula." This means that once (not if) Jordan is taken over by its Palestinian majority, the West Bank Palestinians can become Jordanian citizens who live on Israeli ruled-land. In a July 2012 *New York Times* op-ed, Dayan mathematically "proved" that all 350,000 West Bank settlers are there to stay and concluded, "Instead of lamenting that the status quo is not sustainable, the international community should work together with the parties to improve it where possible and make it more viable." In other words, accept a fait accompli. In mid-2015 Prime Minister Netanyahu rewarded Dayan by appointing him Israel's ambassador to Brazil.

The Israeli-American Neo-Con

Caroline Glick is deputy managing editor of the *Jerusalem Post* and a powerful advocate among American and European neo-conservatives and pro-settler circles. She has no problem offering West Bank Arabs full rights under full annexation because she has solved the demographic problem. There are only 1.5 million Palestinians in the West Bank, not 2.5 million, as all serious demographers—Israeli, Palestinian, international—assert. This reduced demographic figure, which also conveniently ignores the three hundred thousand Palestinian residents of Jerusalem, will be balanced by the immigration to Israel of 1 million Jews from the West—a prediction totally unsupported by experts on the Diaspora—thereby maintaining a Jewish and democratic Israel. Under these circumstances, Glick believes—again, without recognizable foundation in fact—that most of the new Palestinian citizens of Israel will gradually leave in any case.

The Colonialist

Moshe Arens is long retired from politics. He served in the past as minister of defense, minister of foreign affairs, ambassador to Washington, and minister of minorities. In this most minor position of his distinguished career, during the mid-1980s, Arens appears to have honed a suspiciously colonialist-seeming mentality. The key to integrating Arab citizens of Israel into Israeli society, he told me then, is to make them "more like us," meaning more civilized and Western. Once Israel's Arab citizens are better integrated, we can start on the Palestinians in the territories. "Only when [West Bank Arabs] see that Arabs have it good in Israel will they think that this could be good for them as well," he reiterated in 2013. Arens, like others whose political roots go back to the Revisionist Zionist movement (the precursor of the Likud), is fond of quoting Revisionist founder Zeev Jabotinsky to the effect that a Jewish majority of 15 percent would be sufficient to keep Israel a Jewish state and that, while the president would be a Jew, the vice president would be an Arab. (Note that the post of vice president does not exist in the Israeli system.)

The Good Neighbor

Reuven Rivlin, president of the state of Israel since 2014, is a fluent Arabic speaker whose family immigrated to Palestine nearly two hundred years ago and who spent his early years in pre-1948 Jerusalem, with its mix of Jewish and Arab neighborhoods. He is the most senior political figure to have broached the idea of annexing the West Bank and awarding its Arab residents Israeli citizenship. "I prefer that Palestinians be citizens of this state to dividing the land," he has stated, emphasizing that the Land of Israel/Palestine cannot be partitioned because "Jews and Arabs have lived side by side since the dawn of Zionism." Like Arens, Rivlin quotes Jabotinsky about an Arab vice president. Ostensibly, both are adherents of the nineteenth-century liberal values of egalitarianism that originally characterized the Likud but, with few exceptions, no longer do.

But does Rivlin really believe in making Palestinians totally equal Israeli citizens, thereby rendering Israel a state of all its citizens or a binational state? Not quite: he mentions the possibility of "joint sovereignty in Judea and Samaria" under a Jewish state or, alternatively, a vague regime of two parliaments, Jewish and Arab, in a West Bank condominion. Then, too, Rivlin also refers on occasion to a two-state solution, and he acknowledges that Palestinian leader Mahmoud Abbas is a legitimate partner for negotiation. Since taking over the presidency in mid-2014, Rivlin has made a major effort to respect the needs and traditions of Israel's Palestinian Arab population and to advocate conciliation and a pluralistic approach to Israeli life, even when this advocacy brings him into conflict with his original right-wing base. In 2015 he was quoted as stating, "We the children of Abraham must live in the understanding that we are not condemned to live together but rather were meant to live together." He has strongly condemned extremist Jewish right-wing activity in the West Bank. He is undoubtedly the most flexible and creative of the one-state proponents.

The Founder of the Yesha Council

Yisrael Harel believes that "only the Jewish people have a right to sovereignty in the Land of Israel." But he has participated at length in discussions with Arabs from throughout the Middle East and seeks to address realities. At one point a few years ago, he acknowledged that the world might force Israel to accept a two-state partition and even spoke to me of choosing to live in the state of Palestine in order to remain in his home in Ofra (the self-styled "Mayflower" of the settlement movement), near Ramallah. A fallback partition solution from his standpoint is for Areas A and B to become part of Jordan under Palestinian rule, with Area C annexed by Israel.

Despite his demand to annex fully 60 percent of the land in question, Harel is adamant that apartheid is not an issue here in any case: Israel and the Jewish people have no racist prejudices against Arabs; Israel has not legislated separate laws for Jews and Arabs—West Bank Arabs have their own laws as a part of Jordan under Israeli occupation; and whatever restrictions Israel has imposed (and there are many) stem from security needs. Here he seemingly contradicts the point of departure of many of his fellow settlers and settlement supporters, who at least acknowledge that Palestinians are being denied basic rights as a consequence of the occupation.

The Likud Knesset Faction's Right Wing

Three prominent members of the Likud Knesset faction spoke out in early January 2013 in favor of annexing 60 percent of the West Bank or applying Israeli law to all settlements. They are Yuli Edelstein, since 2014 Speaker of the Knesset; Zeev Elkin, in late 2014 chairman of the Knesset Foreign and Security Affairs Committee; and Yariv Levin, chairman of the Likud-led coalition. A fourth, Danny Danon, was on record earlier taking a pro-annexation position. The latter three became ministers in May 2015 in the fourth Netanyahu government, and in August 2015 Prime Minister Netanyahu appointed Danon Israel's ambassador to the United Nations.

Moshe Feiglin, in 2014 a new Likud lawmaker and deputy Knesset Speaker, added his own touch: full annexation and a grant of $500,000 to every Arab family that agrees to emigrate. Elsewhere he has suggested allowing West Bank Arabs to be "permanent residents" of Israel, thereby denying them national rights (Feiglin, a constant rival of Netanyahu within the Likud, lost in the party's primaries in January 2015, thereby forfeiting a Knesset seat).

Tzipi Hotoveli, from May 2015 deputy foreign minister, is another prominent Likud lawmaker in the apartheid camp. Upon taking charge of the Foreign Ministry (in the absence of an appointed minister, she became Israel's senior statesperson), she convened senior Israeli diplomats on May 21 and told them, in a briefing laced with biblical references, "At a time when Israel's very existence is being challenged, it is very important to be just. The international community deals with concepts of morals and justice. In confronting them we must return to the fundamental truth of our right to this land. The entire land is ours. All of it, from the [Mediterranean] sea to the [Jordan] river, and we did not come here to apologize for that."

The Reluctant Security Expert

Retired major general Yaakov Amidror is a brilliant intelligence analyst who famously warned Prime Minister Yitzhak Rabin to beware the duplicity of Yasser Arafat. He later went on to serve as national security adviser to Prime Minister Netanyahu. He favors a two-state solution "for demographic reasons." But he firmly believes Israel has no viable Palestinian partner in the security realm. Accordingly, he prefers to rule over another people, the Palestinians, rather than abandoning Israeli security. In other words, given the security circumstances, he reluctantly prefers a Jewish state to a democratic state. Interestingly, Amidror also advocates Israeli reoccupation of the Gaza Strip—a move that would radically worsen the demographic balance—as the only way to put a stop to repeated Hamas rocket attacks.

It goes without saying that virtually all Palestinians, including those who are Israeli citizens, reject the apartheid-like positions and allusions described here. While West Bank Palestinians who despair of a two-state solution may increasingly be heard advocating their inclusion in a fully binational state or a "state of all its citizens," this position—which, in any case, is anathema to nearly all Israeli Jews—should not be confused with the kind of constrained citizenship rights being offered by the likes of Rivlin, Arens, and Glick.

Nor are any of these apartheid-like positions officially endorsed by Benjamin Netanyahu, Likud party head and prime minister and the principal manipulator of Israeli politics since 2009, or for that matter by a majority of Israelis. Indeed, Netanyahu feels obliged on occasion to reiterate his June 2009 "vision" of "two free peoples living side by side in this small land, with good neighborly relations and mutual respect, each with its flag, anthem and government, with neither one threatening its neighbor's security and existence."

Note that this vision of a two-state solution—voiced at the time to satisfy the Barack Obama administration's urgings—has never been included in the Likud election platform, and many have always doubted Netanyahu's commitment. In the March 2015 elections, he abandoned this position at the last minute to attract extreme right-wing votes: "I think that anyone who is going to establish a Palestinian state today and evacuate lands, is giving attack grounds to radical Islam against the state of Israel." He then "recanted" this rejection of the two-state solution to the international media the day after elections in a maneuver that convinced few international observers.

Official position aside, Netanyahu effectively advances a one-state agenda almost daily with his sponsorship or tolerance of settlement expansion and his total rejection of such core Palestinian (and international) positions as a Palestinian capital in East Jerusalem—in a manner that clearly renders two-state agreement impossible. Accordingly, it is easy to imagine a conversation between Netanyahu and, say, Bennett, in which the prime minister wags his finger and says, "You and I want the same thing in Judea and Samaria. I advance that goal quietly, by expanding settlements even as I play the two-state game of negotiating to lull the international community into gradual acquiescence and find ways to accuse the Palestinians of avoiding peace. I take two steps forward, then stop to accept a temporary freeze until the pressure is off. Then I move forward again, cautiously. You, on the other hand, sabotage our shared goal with your open advocacy of what looks undemocratic and incites international opposition."

By 2015, Netanyahu's enigmatic and ambiguous approach to the two-state issue may have worn thin with most Israeli and international moderates alike. Yet he seemingly continued to believe he would succeed in warding off the international community and the Arab world while still expanding Israel's grip on the West Bank and East Jerusalem and heading Israel's most hawkish government ever.

Thus he could propose to European Union foreign policy chief Federica Mogherini in May 2015 a negotiation of the "borders" of Israel's West Bank settlement blocs as a first step toward a two-state solution, knowing full well that he was obfuscating the border issues with yet another well-intentioned and ill-informed Western potential mediator in order to gain a few months of goodwill and reduce international pressure until, once again, he could point to Palestinian rejection. And he could yet again endorse some sort of broader Arab security envelope that hints ostensibly, and falsely, at Israel's capacity to bypass the Palestinian issue in a turbulent Arab world.

Does Netanyahu know these schemes are ultimately nonstarters? Netanyahu watchers are never quite sure, because Netanyahu never really bares his heart. Every word he speaks publicly, and apparently even privately, is simultaneously sincere and a transparent pose. Here is the Greater Land of Israel ideologist who is slowly, amoeba-like, gobbling up the territories and whose anti–boycott, divestment, and sanctions (BDS) campaign, launched in June 2015 with the support of the American Jewish community, completely ignores the need to explain or end the occupation because BDS is an "anti-Semitic tsunami." Here is the fearmongering leader, now defending Israel against an Iranian Holocaust, now against BDS, now against global anti-Semitism, now using Holocaust-history terminology ("Munich") to castigate Obama for capitulating to Iran.

Here is the heir apparent to Revisionist leader Jabotinsky, now embracing and now discarding such genuine Jabotinsky-style liberals as Beni Begin and Dan Meridor, whose admonishments regarding the rule of law and human rights were once the proud flags of the Likud and today are increasingly the "subversive" lonely protests of the Left and

Center. Yet here also is the ultimate pragmatist who respects Palestinian national rights, awaits a reasonable negotiating partner, froze new settlement starts in the spring of 2015, and is on constant guard against the dangers posed by the binational state bogeyman.

Netanyahu is obviously a very smart politician. He has dealt skillfully with the Arab revolutions in neighboring Syria and Egypt, keeping Israel out of harm's way at a minimal cost. He has shepherded Israel's economy deftly, to the benefit of most Israelis. While he has grossly exaggerated the imminence of the Iranian threat, packaging it in misbegotten Holocaust terminology for maximum effect on Israelis and their supporters in the United States, he can claim considerable credit for persuading the international community to take Iran seriously.

Yet, on the Palestinian issue, he is making mistakes of existential proportions, thereby endangering Israel's Zionist, Jewish, and democratic future. And he has brought Israel to a position where it is daily hemorrhaging American, American Jewish, and particularly European support that it vitally needs.

Netanyahu packages his de facto rejection of withdrawal from the West Bank and East Jerusalem in seemingly genuine fears that Arab and Iranian intentions toward Israel are nothing short of genocidal and that Israel without the territories will be powerless to defend itself. How much of this is genuine, reflecting both real security perceptions and Netanyahu's Revisionist Zionist ideological upbringing, and how much is a pose to justify support for a Greater Land of Israel messianist ideology is another riddle whose solution he carefully guards.

When Netanyahu stated, in response to BDS pressures in June 2015, "It doesn't matter what we do. The struggle against Israel is not connected to our activities: it is connected to our very existence," he was ignoring the very essence of Zionism, which from its earliest days emphasized that Jews could take their fate into their own hands and determine it through their deeds. He was also ignoring Israel's well-proven capacity to defend itself. Then he went out and expanded another settlement in a display of creating facts on the ground that ultimately endanger Israel's security.

It is important also to bear in mind that there are factions of right-wingers who advocate what might be called "creative" two-state solutions that seem divorced from regional and Palestinian realities. Former foreign minister Avigdor Lieberman, for example, whose rhetoric toward Palestinians often sounds racist, wants to pursue a far more ambitious territorial swap than is usually discussed. He would alter the sovereign status of entire regions in Israel that have a large Arab majority so that they become part of a West Bank Palestinian state and, in return, annex large parts of the West Bank. He would presumably oppose a solution that offers any sort of Israeli "rights" to West Bank Palestinians.

Lieberman's concept of repartitioning the land of Mandatory Palestine based on demography enjoys a certain hard territorial-demographic logic. I first broached the same idea in a Jaffee Center study published in late 1994. I suggested it could be one of a number of possible ways to compensate a Palestinian state for Israeli annexation of the West Bank settlement blocs within the framework of a two-state solution. The idea was rejected by Arab citizens of Israel (except Islamists!) and West Bank Palestinians alike. Both insist instead on the 1967 lines and demand that Israeli Arabs remain Israeli citizens living in Israel, not least because they consecrate the land's ultimate Palestinian identity; both reject the notion of Israel being strictly Jewish in its ethnic composition and entertain long-term hopes of "Palestinizing" it by means of Arab population growth and the "return" of 1948 refugees.

In any case, twenty years ago I quickly realized that any attempt to annul the Israeli citizenship of Israeli Arabs living near the green line 1948 boundary, say in Wadi Ara, by moving the borders so their homes were in a Palestinian state would almost certainly be found unconstitutional by the Israel High Court of Justice. Such solutions might have worked after wars in past centuries in Alsace-Lorraine and along the Swiss-Italian border; today they would be judged as depriving persons of their native citizenship in violation of basic human rights.

Then there are those on the left and in the center, as well as a few on the right, who are prepared to conceive of a two-state solution in which upward of one hundred thousand settlers who live outside the settlement blocs abutting the green line remain in place in the West Bank heartland (i.e., inside the Palestinian state). This measure ostensibly would eliminate the need to evacuate them in order to facilitate the emergence of that state, thereby bypassing a major political hurdle for any Israeli government. It would even create a "healthy" symmetry: the presence in Israel of 1.5 million Arab citizens would be "balanced" by the presence in Palestine of a sizeable number of Jews. The settlers, according to this scenario, would wish to remain in the West Bank because of their messianist attachment to the Land of Israel.

Many Palestinians are not necessarily opposed to settlers remaining in Palestine, despite widespread resentment at Israel's settlement landgrab and consequent relegation of Palestinians to second-class status on their own land. But a Palestinian state would inevitably insist that settlers become Palestinian citizens, subject to Palestinian law, including with regard to claims in Palestinian courts regarding the true ownership of disputed land currently included in very prominent settlements. Yet nearly all settlers would only consider remaining behind if their settlements could be Israeli enclaves guarded by themselves and possibly the IDF.

In both cases, the arrangement would quickly degenerate into bloodshed. It would either render the settlers targets of violent Palestinian retribution or create an incentive for settlers to attack their Palestinian neighbors in order to force Israeli security forces to intervene to save Israeli lives, thereby torpedoing the arrangement.

This brings us back to the "classic" two-state solution based on the 1948–1967 green line, with land swaps. It is precisely this solution's presumed feasibility that generates so much opposition on the part of the settlers and their supporters, who covet the land to such an extreme extent or are so convinced that Israel's enemies will use it to attack at virtual point-blank range that they are prepared to compromise either on Israeli democracy or on Israel's Jewish-Zionist character to thwart the emergence of a Palestinian state.

The significance of the quasi-apartheid ideas described here derives from the fact that the camp that advocates them is politically extremely energetic and dynamic, that so many adherents profess to be mainstream, realistic, and nonracist, that some of the advocates are prominent and highly respected, and that in the no-peace and no-process atmosphere prevailing in 2015, their numbers and influence are growing. A reliable December 2014 survey found that about half the Jewish population of Israel favored annexing the territories as a one-state solution (obviously, some of these advocates also say yes when asked if they favor a two-state solution; polls are notoriously flexible). This political reality further isolates Israel internationally and regionally and further erodes the country's democratic underpinnings.

Incidentally, it is interesting to note how quasi-apartheid advocates have seized on the demographic and security ramifications of Israel's 2005 Gaza Strip withdrawal—which they vehemently opposed and have vowed will never be repeated in the West Bank but which freed some 1.7 million Palestinians from most aspects of Israeli control—in order to present schemes in which Jews ostensibly remain a demographic and political majority after annexation of all or most of the West Bank. They want to have their cake and eat it too. On the one hand, they argue, this is doable because without Gaza there are fewer Arabs under Israeli control. On the other hand, they point out, because withdrawal from Gaza has generated a vicious cycle of periodic Palestinian rocket and tunnel attacks against Israeli civilians, withdrawal from the West Bank cannot be contemplated lest it generate a similar outcome.

Here, Netanyahu joins the far right wing by arguing that the danger of rocket and tunnel attacks from the West Bank means, in practical terms, that Israel cannot withdraw its military from there. And that renders meaningless the notion of a sovereign Palestinian state, even if Netanyahu avoids saying so.

Finally, note the link between the Oslo interim division into Areas A, B, and C and the positions advocated by some of the vanguard camp described here. Oslo divided the West Bank as follows: Areas A and B are under variants of Palestinian autonomous control and constitute about 40 percent of the territory, Area C is under Israeli control, and there are separate arrangements for annexed East Jerusalem's Arab inhabitants. But since the Oslo Accords were reached in the mid-1990s, the Oslo process has collapsed into paralysis. It thus created a convenient framework of reference, both for those who now seek to annex Area C (60 percent of the territory) and grant some sort of quasi-apartheid status to Areas A and B and for those who dream of "Palestinizing" the Hashemite Kingdom of Jordan and forcing it to accept Areas A and B (or just their Palestinian residents) as part of that country.

Obviously, this was not the intention of the Oslo signatories. But it offers food for thought regarding the advisability of any additional interim arrangements in the West Bank, East Jerusalem, or elsewhere. They might just end up facilitating Israeli annexation of territories intended by Oslo and the international community for Palestinian rule. This is precisely what the Palestinian leadership in the West Bank fears when confronting Israeli proposals for partial unilateral withdrawal.

TEN

Summarizing the Strategic Ramifications of the Quasi-Apartheid Schemes

The right-wing schemes discussed here fall into several categories or models. At one extreme of the spectrum is a genuine binational state model in which all Arabs in East Jerusalem and the West Bank receive full and unqualified Israeli citizenship without regard to their ideological inclinations. As we have seen, none of the right-wing advocates really believe in this option; the most liberal proffer conditions for citizenship such as allegiance to Israel as a Zionist state, gradual absorption based on acceptable political behavior, and so forth. Meanwhile, right-wing Jewish nationalists actually seek to water down the national and civic rights of Israel's own Palestinian Arab citizens and to deny equal socioeconomic status to Arab East Jerusalem residents.

Further, while there are already Israeli Arab judges and diplomats, tycoons and scholars, few Israelis will really willingly adopt a binational model that places key aspects of their economic well-being and physical security in the hands of Arab ministers. An Arab minister of defense with control over Israel's nuclear capabilities? An Arab chief of police or minister of housing? These options would not necessarily appeal even to the small left-wing so-called post-Zionist Jewish camp that advocates a binational state. Such a model, being by definition non-Zionist, would inevitably precipitate the mass departure of those Jews able to leave and the rapid emergence of an Arab state with a dwindling Jewish minority.

At the other end of the spectrum are two options. One annexes Area C and awards its small Arab population full Israeli citizenship, or perhaps residency rights as in East Jerusalem, and consigns the population of the rest of the West Bank to autonomy status or Jordanian citizenship.

Note that close to half of Jordan's population is already Palestinian—a proportion reduced in recent years by the influx of non-Palestinian refugees, first from Iraq and most recently from Syria. Most Palestinian refugees who fled in 1948 to Jordan enjoy Jordanian citizenship and prominence in the business sector but are generally prevented from reaching positions of political or security authority. Note, too, that the Israeli security establishment has every interest in Jordan remaining stable and relatively friendly toward Israel—meaning, in the Middle East reality, non-Palestinian.

Needless to say, Hashemite Jordan will not cooperate with the scheme whereby Israel annexes Area C. Jordan will not provide Jordanian citizenship to the vast majority of West Bank Palestinians in Areas A and B, thereby enlarging its own Palestinian population to unmanageable proportions. In other words, this option allocates second-class status to most, if not all, West Bank Palestinians.

A variation on this option proposes, somehow, to Palestinize the Hashemite Kingdom of Jordan—that is, to render it a Palestinian rather than a Hashemite state—and then to oblige it to award full citizenship status to West Bank Palestinians, who would continue to live under autonomy or even in territory annexed to Israel while holding Jordanian passports and voting in Jordanian elections. One obvious problem with this idea is that the Hashemite establishment in Amman would not agree—it wants to remain Hashemite—and would have to be overthrown. A second is that even a Palestinized Jordan might not agree to make life easy for Israel by offering its citizenship to West Bank Arabs.

Further, Jordan (now Palestine) would cease to be a tacit security ally of Israel and to offer it a vital degree of strategic depth to its east and a buffer against Iraq and to some extent Syria—all states hostile to Israel where militant Sunnis and Iran-backed Shiites were running rampant in 2015. Jordan would become an enemy state located just across the Jordan River, potentially offering hostile access to Israel to implacable enemies like Iran. Or worse, if the East Bank Palestinian state (formerly Jordan) also comprised Areas A and B of the West Bank, as some advocate, Israel would confront a potentially extremist Palestinian state with a huge score to settle—a state beginning some fifteen to twenty kilometers from the Mediterranean and ending at the Iraqi border.

Significantly, hawkish Israeli prime ministers like Yitzhak Shamir and Ariel Sharon, who rose to power advocating the Palestinization of Jordan as a means of holding onto the West Bank, changed their minds once, from the pinnacle of the premiership in Jerusalem, they recognized how strategically important Hashemite Jordan is as a neighbor to Israel. Jordan as constituted offers Israel vital strategic depth to the east and a shared strategic approach to the Islamist threat emanating from Iraq and Syria. A Palestinized Jordan would conceivably move that threat right up to Israel's eastern borders.

A second option annexes all of the West Bank and allocates to its Arab residents some form of second-class citizenship status: individual rights, perhaps even communal rights, but no national rights unless they choose of their own volition to opt in favor of Jordanian citizenship and Jordan agrees, which it won't.

There is not really a great deal of difference among all these options and variations. Israel directly rules all or most of the land and militarily controls all of it. Arabs, Palestinian or Israeli, do not have full national rights. Some West Bankers may be able to obtain Israeli citizenship and join the ranks of the Arab citizens of Israel who, because they refuse to acquiesce in the Jewish-Zionist character of the state, are "rewarded" with inadequate municipal budgets and dwindling land rights but can avail themselves of superior opportunities for education and enterprise and have full recourse to the independent Israeli judicial system. Most West Bankers will probably reject this option—in the unlikely event that it is offered to them.

So it all boils down to one form or another of apartheid, or rule by Israeli Jews over a nearly equivalent number of Palestinian Arabs who enjoy varying degrees of personal and perhaps even communal rights but few, if any, national rights. Israel will be less Jewish and less democratic but more messianist. As matters stand, this could be the situation within a decade or two.

What will happen then? Here are several possible scenarios, not all necessarily mutually exclusive.

2025, SCENARIO 1: THE CURRENT NEGATIVE DIRECTION PREVAILS

The reality will be far from tranquil. Agitation for a two-state solution, by Israelis and Palestinians alike, will dwindle and disappear. The West Bank will be increasingly rendered semiautonomous with severe limitations. Virtually all classes of Palestinian Arabs—Israeli citizens, East Jerusalem–based residents of Israel, residents of annexed Area C of the West Bank, and residents of Areas A and B—will proceed to agitate for totally equal rights in a binational state. Some will use violence; others will seek support from neighboring Arab states, Europe, and the United Nations.

Suppression of Palestinian terrorism will increasingly be seen as a critical internal Israeli civil and human rights issue rather than a by-product of Israeli occupation. The distinction between terrorism and legitimate expressions of opposition to Israeli rule—already in 2015 a problematic concept—will be increasingly obfuscated. Israel will have united all Palestinians against it. No part of Israel—now reaching either de facto or de jure from the Mediterranean Sea to the Jordan River—will be free of violence. The Israel Defense Forces (IDF), long obliged by occupation duties to fill policing tasks in the occupied territories, will now encounter a total blur between war fighting and domestic policing and a conflation of its scope of activity with that of the Israel Police. The Gaza Strip—not included in these new arrangements—will for the nth time launch a rocket and tunnel war against Israel in support of Palestinian rights and the elimination of the state of Israel. Jerusalem's Temple Mount will be a focus of tension. Tourism will decline drastically.

If we are looking for a model elsewhere in the region that helps us better understand the direction Israel takes, it will be Lebanon—albeit "on steroids."

Why Lebanon? Because Israel's northern neighbor is the closest model we can find in the Middle East for what Israel will become. That country's polity is based on a weak and constantly failing political system that awards a measure of representation to each of nineteen different ethno-religious groups and lurches from crisis to crisis, with internal violence and interference by neighbors a constant and with the largest "tribe," the Shiites, increasingly dominant.

And why on steroids? Because the Israeli version will leave power in the hands of only one ethno-religious group—itself seriously fragmented between secular and religious, right and left, settler supporters and the secular liberal "state of Tel Aviv"—while denying power to the other in varying degrees (Israeli Arab citizens will have more, West Bankers less, and so forth). Whereas in Lebanon a series of intercommunal crises has repeatedly generated "tweaks" to the representation system that have enabled the continued existence of a modicum of quiet (if unstable) coexistence, in Israel the system will offer little at all by way of a political process for dealing with grievances.

Indeed, this reality will serve to reinforce the fallacious Palestinian narrative that Israel is a colonialist, imperialist entity that does not represent a genuine people embracing a legitimate national movement. Palestinian textbooks already portray the conflict as akin to that in Algeria, where a colonialist oppressor, France, was eventually forced out by the violence of a civil war. Now, Israel will be seen as fulfilling this distorted comparison. Accordingly, violence will be far worse than in Lebanon precisely because Israel does not really fit this narrative and because, over recent decades in Lebanon, Arab powers Saudi Arabia and Syria could at crucial junctures impose new arrangements for governance.

Israel will have no such helpful neighbor. The reaction to these developments on the part of the rest of the Middle East and the international community will be critical. Assuming they themselves are not overrun by militant Islam, Jordan and Egypt may end up having little choice but reluctantly and at the risk of their own security to reassess their peace-treaty-based security ties with Israel lest their own publics and their neighbors come to view their leaders as quislings. The rest of the Arab world might remain passive—it is liable to be preoccupied with its own dysfunctional nature for years to come—but it almost certainly won't be available openly to make common cause with Israel against shared enemies like Iran and militant jihadists.

As for the United States and Europe, this apartheid-like dynamic in Israel will fuel Western disenchantment with the (no longer democratic) Jewish state. In the United States, a persistent camp of Jewish hard-liners, egged on by those who, like billionaire Sheldon Adelson, have no real problem with a less-than-democratic Israel as long as it can claim to be Jewish, will join with messianist Christian evangelicals and Republican hard-liners to continue to support Israel and to advocate American financial and security support, which nevertheless could decrease.

But Israel will begin to lose the adherence of much of the American Jewish Diaspora, which will find it impossible to maintain enthusiastic backing for a country that does not reflect its basic values. This presages a split in the Jewish world without precedent since Israel was founded in 1948 and a genuine crisis of identity for the American Jewish community. And beyond the Jewish world, Israel will increasingly lose the civilized world as its policies fuel the boycott, divestment, and sanctions (BDS) campaign.

Indeed, with the West Bank increasingly swallowed by Israel, the hard core of the BDS movement that condemns Israel's very existence will become increasingly dominant over those who profess merely to oppose the occupation. If, in May 2015, the Palestinians nearly succeeded in suspending Israel from the International Federation of Association Football (FIFA), the world football (American soccer) federation, because it fields teams in West Bank settlements, now the Palestinians may ultimately petition FIFA to demand that Israel incorporate their teams into a joint, binational federation more in keeping with the times.

Europe, where BDS is already more strongly rooted and where the often anti-Semitic influence of a prolonged Muslim immigration wave grows more persistent by the year, will ratchet up the economic and political sanctions, which already in 2015 reflected the European Union demand that Israel advance the two-state solution and respect EU human rights standards. Israel will find a degree of solace in the crippling effect on this dynamic generated by EU disunity and the need of European intelligence services to maintain close links with Israeli intelligence precisely because of the Islamist threat. Then, too, right-wing Israelis will take a leaf from Russia's Vladimir Putin, who in 2015 was still successfully defying EU sanctions over his creeping takeover of parts of Ukraine. In other words, as with the United States, enough channels of commerce and communication will remain open with Europe to dispel the notion of a total break.

Still, the sense of jarring dissonance between Israel on the one hand and its Jewish links and civilizational roots in the West on the other will be a growing source of alarm. This dynamic will also accelerate Israel's pivot—already glaringly evident by 2015 under Benjamin Netanyahu's leadership—toward greater economic integration with the East: Russia, India, and China, all of which are less discriminating than the West when it comes to human rights in Israel or anywhere else. Yet none of these countries can replace what the West gives Israel: not only economic prosperity but also a sense of cultural, political, and religious identity.

If the current direction prevails, this is the Israel we are likely to encounter by 2025: increasingly isolated from most of the West and most of Western and especially American Jewry; poorer economically and intellectually; more and more inwardly focused with a siege mentality; thoroughly dominated by nationalistic, right-religious Jewish factions; and increasingly the locus of internal Arab-Jewish conflict and the target of external enmity.

Some European Jews, fleeing Islamist pressure, might still come and invest, alongside Russian oligarchs and Chinese seeking to buy up intellectual property. But an exodus of Jews who refuse to live in such a narrow, conflicted state will more than neutralize their numbers. Natural gas and water for desalination drawn from the country's Mediterranean strategic depth will help keep the economy afloat. Those on the political Right who sincerely believe there is no better alternative will advocate measures like "improving the status quo" (read: economic peace) until, they believe, the Palestinians come to their senses. Meanwhile, Tel Aviv's famously vibrant economic, intellectual, and cultural "bubble" will shrink apace, and at least a portion of the high-tech engine that drives the economy will consider relocating abroad.

A useful comparison might be Taiwan. Living in the shadow of the People's Republic of China (PRC), its ambassador-level diplomatic relations reduced to a handful of countries and its sovereign independence and legitimacy questioned by most of the world, it nevertheless continues to prosper economically and to innovate on the cutting edge of information technology. The threat to Taiwan's security lies in Beijing; the guarantor of its security is the United States, without which it has no chance to survive if the PRC decides to take charge. While in 2025 Israel will be far more capable militarily, it will also strongly desire American security guarantees. And it will presumably continue to have more and more varied Sunni and Shiite enemies, including a Palestinian threat from within.

Indeed, Palestinian demographic and security pressure, now centered almost entirely inside the country, will grow. Iran and, separately, a variety of Islamist-dominated states, egged on by Washington's ongoing policy mistakes in the region, might now be tempted to launch a major attack or series of attacks on Israel. In the event of war, Tel Aviv will no longer be able to rely automatically on key dimensions of its military-strategic preparedness, such as rapid arms resupply by the United States and the capacity to maintain stability and quiet on the home front. The

Israeli-American security relationship, for decades an indispensable pillar of Israeli strategic thinking, will be increasingly imperiled.

2025, SCENARIO 2: THE REST OF THE ARABS ARE INCREASINGLY FED UP WITH PALESTINIAN OBSTINACY

Will it really be that bad? Here a word of caution is in order. As we saw in looking at pre-1967 Israel, the country has known acute isolation, sanctions, and repressive internal measures before and has overcome them and emerged stronger and healthier. Israel will remain better off in a military-strategic sense than in its early decades, when every war posed the specter of the state's collapse or conquest. By 2015, far-reaching security relationships with Egypt and Jordan and intelligence relationships with additional Arab countries, however clandestine, attested to the perception among some Arab regimes that Israel is a strategic asset.

Is it entirely beyond the realm of possibility that a courageous Arab leader, hitherto Israel's declared enemy, will, observing the chaos and militant Islam sweeping the region, unexpectedly opt for some sort of rapprochement with Israel, despite the festering sore of the Palestinian issue? Could Israel's Arab state neighbors demand that the Palestinians acquiesce in interim arrangements, partial withdrawals, some sort of temporary peace (*hudna*, an Arab concept) that doesn't satisfy all Palestinian demands? Stranger things have happened in the Middle East.

2025, SCENARIO 3: ISRAELIS COME TO THEIR SENSES

Meanwhile, the Israeli public continues to vote in democratic elections — a factor militating against any inclination to draw hasty conclusions and write off Israel as a Jewish and democratic entity. Some Israeli liberals are already rationalizing the current direction of events as the only one that will eventually bring Israelis to their senses: once the messianist right wing sees how much damage it has done, it will take the initiative to withdraw, even unilaterally, and establish a Palestinian state, with few left on the political spectrum to oppose the move. In other words, in a Leninist mode, the worse things become, the more likely they will be to somehow usher in revolutionary change.

The Yom Kippur War of 1973, with its huge Israeli losses, could be considered a prototype for this sort of cataclysmic and traumatic event. It was preceded by indifference to a deteriorating situation and a false sense of well-being. It was followed by radical change, including a successful peace process with Egypt.

According to this reading, Israelis will finally understand that it is better to confront a problematic Palestinian neighbor in the West Bank and Gaza and to maintain "little Israel" as a Jewish and democratic state than to swallow the West Bank with its entire Palestinian population and face Israel's rapid metamorphosis into a binational, apartheid state. Better even, in a worst-case scenario, to contemplate rockets launched from the West Bank against civilians in Tel Aviv and aircraft at Ben Gurion Airport, followed by yet another punitive military expedition to Ramallah and Jenin backed by massive national unity and public approval of the government's actions—the pattern that has developed vis-à-vis the Gaza Strip—than to live in a state so badly conflicted within itself that no one needs to attack it for it to disintegrate.

2025, SCENARIO 4: PALESTINIAN REVOLT

As stalemate prevails year after year, a mass movement sweeps the West Bank and East Jerusalem. It could be violent—a third intifada—or it could involve peaceful demonstrations. The movement demands official annulment of the by now totally defunct Oslo Accords and dismantlement of the Palestinian Authority (PA). It might also demand Israeli citizenship for nearly 3 million West Bank and East Jerusalem Palestinians (and in principle for another 2 million in the Gaza Strip, where the demand and protest ring hollow in view of the lack of an Israeli presence and the strong arm of Hamas rule). It could provoke demonstrations of support among Arab citizens of Israel. Here, for example, is Palestine Liberation Organization (PLO) chief negotiator Saeb Erekat in mid-June 2015: "Israel will have to make a choice before the end of this year: Either we have a contract and partnership that will lead to a two-state solution, or Israel will be solely responsible [for the areas and the people] from the Jordan River to the Mediterranean."

That this scenario has not emerged until now (Erekat has a well-known penchant for delivering ultimatums that fail to materialize on time) appears to reflect three factors. One is a vested interest in the status quo demonstrated by tens of thousands of PA employees, hundreds of thousands more who have prospered under PA rule, and East Jerusalem Palestinians who are relatively well-off. A second is fear that, without security cooperation between PA forces and Israel, Islamist extremists will take over the Area A Palestinian cities, eliminate the PA/PLO leaders, and Islamize what was in 2015 a fairly easygoing way of life. And a third is fear of Israeli military reaction: the IDF retaking full control of the West Bank.

On the other hand, no one in Israel desires reoccupation, with its financial costs and the international stigma and condemnation it would invite. And few Israelis would opt for awarding Israeli citizenship across the board. Accordingly, under this scenario Israel would probably apply "creative" stopgap measures such as annexing Area C and "imposing" autonomy on Areas A and B, possibly with additional wishful-thinking provisions for some limited form of Israeli citizenship to be awarded on a selective basis in accordance with right-wing proposals for a one-state solution. In other words, this scenario would not remain static for long.

2025, SCENARIO 5: PALESTINIAN ACQUIESCENCE

As the Israeli pro-settler Right gains more power and seeks to impose its vision on the West Bank, is it possible the Palestinians of Nablus, Ramallah, and Hebron will give up their independence struggle and come to see themselves as living relatively placidly in what would be viewed as a friendly autonomy rather than a nasty Bantustan—what veteran *Haaretz* Palestine correspondent Amira Hass terms the "vision of seven states," referring to the Gaza Strip and the diverse Area A municipal enclaves (Hebron, Bethlehem, Ramallah, and so forth) in the West Bank? Will East Jerusalem's hundreds of thousands of Palestinians prefer their status as permanent residents of Israel, with all the material advantages this provides, rather than agitating for the eastern part of the city to become the capital of the sovereign state of Palestine in a violent and dysfunctional Arab Middle East?

Will coexistence prevail on the Temple Mount? Could the PLO yield representation of West Bank Palestinians to a more moderate faction that emphasizes the economic advantages and relative stability of being Israel's second-class citizens or semiautonomous neighbors? This is what some pro-settler circles confidently predict—if only all other concerned parties would agree to look the other way and treat Israel with benign neglect. In other words, economic peace triumphs.

Scenario 1 is the most likely to materialize, scenario 5 the least likely. The combination of political domination by a messianist settler-led branch of Judaism, angry Palestinian opposition and chronic dysfunction, traditional (and, sadly, sometimes justified) Jewish fears of persecution, and life in a really bad neighborhood will be devastating. Israel will increasingly behave like its tribalized neighbors. Palestine will officially be deemed a state in the eyes of the United Nations and many countries in the world, but in reality it will comprise a number of violent, disjointed, and semiautonomous enclaves (including Gaza and West Bank Areas A and B), the status of its residents increasingly muddled, surrounded by Israel in the midst of an unstable and crisis-ridden Middle East.

Certainly, one key factor pervades all the scenarios: internal discord, violence, and repression inside expanded Israel cannot be confined to that small country; these phenomena will affect the region and, indeed, the international scene. This means that Israel's problem is also the region's problem, Europe's problem, America's problem, and American Jewry's problem. It means that Israel's West Bank policies over nearly fifty years add up to a strategic mistake worthy of being listed in Barbara Tuchman's 1984 *March of Folly* alongside the Trojan War and the US war in Vietnam. It means that maverick Israeli philosopher Yeshayahu Leibowitz was right when he foresaw decades ago an Israel beset by "the corruption characteristic of every colonial regime" and predicted "the liquidation of the State of Israel as the state of the Jewish people." And it means that Israel's current phantom well-being—a booming economy, ties with Arab neighbors, strong political and economic counteroffensives against international boycott campaigns that seem to display more noise than substance—will soon inevitably be crumbling at the edges.

If this assessment is valid, all these regional, international, and Jewish actors must begin to consider how they are going to adapt to a future increasingly likely to be characterized by the absence of a solution and a creeping apartheid reality in Israel-Palestine. How can they prevent destabilizing spillover effects on the region, particularly among Jordan's ethnic Palestinian majority? How will the American Jewish mainstream define its underlying values when confronted by a nondemocratic Israel?

And if this assessment is in fact valid, the relevant think tanks and research institutes in Israel and everywhere else must consider altering their agendas. Instead of pondering improved formulae for an elusive peace process, they should begin to look at the modalities of Israel's future behavior under extreme duress and adversity, along with the strategic ramifications for Israel itself of its increasingly negative regional and international status as the occupation approaches fifty years. Will partial measures to lower the profile of the conflict still be viable? How will Israeli chaos interact with Arab chaos?

Still, as emphasized in the brief conclusion that follows, in Israel's part of the world, nothing is written in stone.

ELEVEN

Are There Radical
Alternative Realities?

The United Nations Special Coordinator (UNSCO) for the Middle East Peace Process is based at the old British High Commissioner's residence, which lies roughly between East and West Jerusalem on the hilltop known since biblical times by the grimly appropriate name of "the Hill of Evil Counsel." Prior to 1967, when Israel captured Arab East Jerusalem, the residence symbolized the divide between Israel and Jordan/Palestine—the very same divide that underlies "Rachel," the story that opens this book.

UNSCO was created in 1994 to help shepherd the Oslo process. Accordingly, in the eyes of most Israelis and Palestinians, it cannot be credited with having accomplished very much. Still, its spokesperson issues a daily press brief, which offers a useful roundup of what UNSCO deems the relevant conflict-related news of the day.

Here is a prominent and typical entry from Thursday, March 26, 2015:

> EU urges quick restart to Israeli-Palestinian talks: The European Union urged Israelis and Palestinians on Wednesday to quickly restart peace talks that collapsed last year, as the bloc's new foreign policy chief seeks to reinvigorate European involvement in the negotiations. Israel should make "every effort to ensure an early resumption of the Middle East peace process," the EU said in a series of annual reports assessing progress on democracy and human rights in countries close to the 28-nation bloc. A separate report urged the Palestinian Authority to pursue "positive steps" to restart peace talks. In its reports, the EU called on Israel to ensure respect for international law and human rights in the occupied territories. While the EU recognized Israel had the right to defend itself, the "devastating effect" of last year's Gaza conflict on civilians "underlined the significant challenges attached to Israel's re-

sponsibilities in the occupied territories," it said. The EU also urged the
Palestinian Authority to resume full governmental responsibility in
Gaza and to organize free and fair presidential and legislative elections.
(Reuters).

You read this bulletin, scratch your head, and ask whether the European Union officials who deal with the conflict and the United Nations officials who put that EU bulletin in their daily brief live on the same planet as most Israelis and Palestinians. Yet this bulletin seemingly encapsulates the good intentions and good wishes of many peace-minded circles and senior statesmen and politicians in the international community. Nor are statements emanating from the United States radically different. In April–May 2015, both National Security Adviser Susan Rice and Undersecretary of State Wendy Sherman warned Israel that the government that emerges from its March elections must recommit to the two-state solution. They were responding to Benjamin Netanyahu's seeming renunciation of that solution just before elections, which he in any case promptly retracted—as if these verbal exercises still impress any of the players.

At least President Barack Obama acknowledged in mid-May 2015 that there was no chance for a process in the coming year due to Netanyahu's positions and Mahmoud Abbas's "challenges." But then he proceeded to fall back on an economic peace formula as a stopgap. It seems that the concepts and perceptions underlying the launch by Secretary of State John Kerry of the ill-advised peace process in July 2013 are still very much alive in Washington. Lord Peel wrote in 1937, "Partition offers a chance of ultimate peace. No other plan does." As yet, few on the international scene seem prepared to contemplate the possibility that there is no ultimate peace.

If the insights presented in this book make sense, then the primary advocates of a two-state solution on the international scene are seriously deluding themselves and the world. If, however, the concepts informing the EU bulletin, the Rice and Sherman statements, and the Kerry peace initiative correspond with reality, then matters are not nearly as dismal and negative as I understand them to be. All we Israelis and Palestinians really need is another push.

Perhaps—a third alternative reality—the European Union and the United States are wildly unrealistic, my analysis is simply too logical and rational (meaning not at all Middle Eastern), and a deus ex machina can be counted on to appear and radically scramble the picture. Who anticipated the 1967 Six-Day War that changed the face of the Middle East? Who expected Anwar Sadat to invite himself to Jerusalem in November 1977? Who predicted the fall of the Soviet Union, Saddam Hussein's invasion of Kuwait, the Oslo breakthrough, and the so-called Arab Spring with its cascading collapse of Arab regimes?

Who can possibly predict what course the Middle East, Israel included, will take in the coming ten years? Will King Salman of Saudi Arabia invite himself to Jerusalem? Will an Israeli-Iranian war be so devastating as to force us all to rethink everything? Will a horrific massacre of civilians—perpetrated by a Palestinian against Israelis, or by an Israeli against Palestinians—completely reshuffle the deck?

The analysis and projections offered in this book are my best guess as to where current trends in the conflict and in Israeli political behavior and Palestinian dysfunctionality will take us. Reality could well be different: possibly better, possibly worse.

These thoughts are also a call for context and perspective. Lest we forget, the occupation that began in June 1967 was part and parcel of a major military victory over Arab enemies that sought Israel's destruction and demise—a high point in the country's history. Whatever happens in the Israeli-Palestinian sphere, Israel will hopefully still have a great deal to offer—to itself, the region, the Jewish people, and the world.

When last I checked, the two cousins Hajar and Shlomit were still in contact, still vying to overcome the obstacles to a direct meeting, so that they might finally see one another face to face.

Index

About the Author

Yossi Alpher is a former official in the Mossad and former director of the Jaffee Center for Strategic Studies at Tel Aviv University. Alpher's fifty years of experience in dealing with the Palestinian issue include his intelligence career, landmark research while at the Jaffee Center on recognition of the PLO, the two-state solution and the borders and settlements issues, the *bitterlemons* digital dialogue project, extensive facilitation of informal Israeli-Palestinian dialogue, and a stint as special adviser to Prime Minister Ehud Barak during the July 2000 Camp David talks.

Alpher has written extensively in both English and Hebrew on Israel-related strategic issues. In January 2015 he published *Periphery: Israel's Search for Middle East Allies*, described by *The Guardian* as "sparkling" and "a torrent of fresh air."